The 5-Minute
BIBLE
STUDY
for
Women

ISBN 978-1-68322-656-7

Published by Barbour Books, an imprint of Barbour Publishing, Inc., 1810 Barbour Drive, Uhrichsville, Ohio 44683, www.barbourbooks.com

Our mission is to inspire the world with the life-changing message of the Bible.

Member of the
Evangelical Christian
Publishers Association

Printed in the United States of America.

The 5-Minute
BIBLE
STUDY
for
Women

EMILY BIGGERS

BARBOUR BOOKS
An Imprint of Barbour Publishing, Inc.

INTRODUCTION

Do you find it hard to make time for Bible study? You intend to do it, but the hours turn into days and before you know it, another week has passed and you have not picked up God's Word. This book provides an avenue for you to open the Bible regularly and dig into a passage—even if you only have five minutes!

Minutes 1–2: *Read* carefully the scripture passage for each day's Bible study.

Minute 3: *Understand.* Ponder a couple of prompts designed to help you apply the verses from the Bible to your own life. Consider these throughout your day as well.

Minute 4: *Apply.* Read a brief devotion based on the day's scripture. Think about what you are learning and how to apply the scriptural truths to your own life.

Minute 5: *Pray.* A prayer starter will help you to begin a time of conversation with God. Remember to allow time for Him to speak into your life as well.

May *The 5-Minute Bible Study for Women* help you to establish the discipline of studying God's Word. Pour yourself a cup of coffee and make that first five minutes of your day count! You will find that even a few minutes focused on scripture and prayer has the power to make a huge difference. Soon you will want to spend even more time in God's Word!

A CREATIVE CREATOR
Read Genesis 1:1–31

Key Verse:

God saw all that he had made, and it was very good. And there was evening, and there was morning—the sixth day.
GENESIS 1:31 NIV

Understand:

- *Consider the intricate details seen in nature. The petals of a flower that are arranged in a set pattern. The perfect curve of a nautilus shell. The instincts of a lion. Think of three examples of your own.*

- *If the world came about after a "Big Bang," as some scientists say, how could the detail seen in nature be explained?*

Apply:

The book of Genesis begins with the words "In the beginning God created. . . ." If God was already creating *in the beginning*, then that means He was not Himself created, but rather, He is the great Creator of all things.

God separated day from night. He made the stars, moon, and sun. He created the many varieties of trees and flowers, each one intricate in its design!

God made all of the animals—the unique hippo and giraffe, the enormous elephant and whale, the majestic lion. . . . God is a creative Creator!

God's greatest creations were made in His image. Men, women, and children are special to God. We bear some of His traits. We are His masterpieces.

Remember to notice the details of God's glorious creation as you go about your day. Take care of the earth. It was designed by your Father. Respect all other people. They, like you, bear the image of God.

Heavenly Father, You have made all things. You are the Creator who sustains life. You knit me together in my mother's womb. May I treat with great respect all of Your creation, even that which others may devalue. In Jesus' name I pray. Amen.

....

....

....

....

....

....

....

....

....

TEMPTATION
Read Genesis 3:1–24

Key Verse:

Now the serpent was more crafty than any of the wild animals the Lord God had made. He said to the woman, "Did God really say, 'You must not eat from any tree in the garden'?"
Genesis 3:1 niv

Understand:

- *Have you ever tried to rationalize a sin that you know you are committing against God?*

- *What will you do the next time Satan tempts you to disobey God?*

Apply:

Satan appears as a serpent in Genesis 3. He tempts the first people, as he tempts believers today, in a sneaky manner.

Adam and Eve had heard God clearly. He had given them free rein in the garden. They could eat of any tree *except* one. He had not restricted them in a harsh way. They had great freedom. They were given one rule, one tree to avoid, one guideline to obey.

Satan was crafty in his approach, wasn't he? He uses this technique with believers today as well. Use caution if you begin to think to yourself: *Does God really have such a guideline for my life? Would He really limit me in this way? Is this really a sin? Is it really so bad?*

God's standards and His rules are for our good. He has drawn boundary lines for us in pleasant places (see Psalm 16:6). Don't let Satan tempt you to believe otherwise.

God, I am sorry for rationalizing sin. I try to find a way to make sin okay, but sin is never to be swept under the rug. Help me to walk in Your ways and to recognize sin as sin. Please give me strength to withstand temptation. In Jesus' name I pray. Amen.

....

....

....

....

....

....

....

....

....

....

....

NEVER LOOK BACK
Read Genesis 19:1–26

Key Verse:

But Lot's wife looked back, and she became a pillar of salt.
GENESIS 19:26 NIV

Understand:

- *After becoming a believer, have you ever been tempted to "look back" at something Jesus called you to lay down? What was it? How did you respond to the temptation?*

- *Why do you think God imposed such a harsh punishment on Lot's wife just for looking back as she was leaving Sodom?*

Apply:

Not unlike the call to evacuate before a hurricane (although much stronger!), Lot's family received a warning from angels to get out of Sodom before God destroyed the entire city.

Lot's wife, a Sodomite, looked back as they were leaving. On her way out of the city, the memory of sinful pleasures she had enjoyed there cost her everything. Like the lure of a county fair's music and the scrumptious scent of delicious foods, Sodom beckoned her. Just one glance back was all she took.

But it was enough for our holy God to turn her instantly into a pillar of salt.

Don't spend time looking back. Whether it's past sin that calls your name or a past relationship or status, resist the urge to dwell in the past. A wise man once said, "If you live in the past, you will miss the present, and therefore you will have no future."

God provided an escape route from sin. His name is Jesus. Follow Him, and never look back.

Pray:

Heavenly Father, I pray that You will keep me from the snares of temptation. May my eyes be so focused on Your will and Your ways for my life that I might never look back. You have promised me hope and a future (see Jeremiah 29:11). Please never let my heart stray from Your best for me. Amen.

....

....

....

....

....

....

....

....

....

FEAR GOD ABOVE MAN

Read Exodus 1:1–22

Key Verse:

But the nurses feared God, so they did not do as the king told them; they let all the boy babies live.
EXODUS 1:17 NCV

Understand:

- *When is it right to disobey civil leaders?*

- *What did God do for the two midwives of Exodus 1 because they feared Him?*

Apply:

Shiphrah and Puah. They are not names mentioned at the average family's dinner table! Have you heard of them? As we read Exodus 1, we find that these two midwives are the heroines of the story! They were told to kill the Israelites' baby boys as soon as they were born. They feared God more than they feared the possibility of being caught disobeying the law of the land. They knew that God created and valued the life of each baby—Egyptian or Israelite. They had a holy reverence for life. After all, their job was to help women deliver their babies.

God does not want us to disobey the leaders of our government; however, there are times when this is the right choice. Pray that you would be as wise as Shiphrah and Puah to know the difference between times when you should submit to authority and times when you should not. As a believer, if something goes against God, you are not to do it even if your leader calls you to.

Pray:

Lord, thank You for the boldness of the two midwives who knew what the king ordered was wrong. They chose life! Thank You for the opportunities I have to do what is right even when it may be hard or frightening. May I be as bold as Shiphrah and Puah if following You becomes as dangerous for me as it was for them. Amen.

....

....

....

....

....

....

....

....

....

....

I AM
Read Exodus 3:1–22

Key Verses:

Moses said to God, "Suppose I go to the Israelites and say to them, 'The God of your fathers has sent me to you,' and they ask me, 'What is his name?' Then what shall I tell them?"

God said to Moses, "I am who I am. This is what you are to say to the Israelites: 'I am has sent me to you.'"
EXODUS 3:13–14 NIV

Understand:

- *Moses questioned God. Does it appear that God was patient with Moses' questions or that Moses' insecurities angered God? Is it okay to bring your questions to God?*

- *What do you think God meant when He referred to Himself as "I Am?"*

Apply:

God was not worried, or taken aback, by the question. He told Moses to tell the Israelites he had been sent by "I am."

God's essence is not containable in human language. No word or phrase can describe Him. "I am" signifies that God indeed *exists*. He is *different* from all other life. He *was*, *is*, and *will be*.

Whatever the Israelites needed on their exodus from Egypt, God *was*. He parted the Red Sea at just the necessary moment and yet allowed it to swallow up their pursuers. He led them by fire and by cloud. He provided water for their parchedness. He showered them with daily bread.

If there is one thing we know about our Lord, it is that He is unchanging. He is the same yesterday, today, and forever (see Hebrews 13:8). The Great "I AM" stands ready to meet your needs today just as He did for the Israelites.

Pray:

Great I AM, I humbly ask You to take the reins and lead me day to day, step by step through life, just as You led your people out of slavery in the land of Egypt. Amen.

....

....

....

....

....

....

....

....

....

....

MIRIAM'S CELEBRATION
Read Exodus 15:1–27

Key Verses:

Then Miriam the prophetess, the sister of Aaron, took the timbrel in her hand; and all the women went out after her with timbrels and with dances. And Miriam answered them:
"Sing to the LORD,
For He has triumphed gloriously!
The horse and its rider
He has thrown into the sea!"
EXODUS 15:20–21 NKJV

Understand:

- *Miriam was the older sister of Moses. Read Exodus 2 as a reminder of the backstory. What had Miriam done to save Moses' life?*

- *What has God done in your life that you can take time to celebrate today?*

Apply:

Miriam watched as the Egyptians were swallowed up by the Red Sea. She had crossed over on dry land. She had witnessed the miracle. But this was not all she celebrated as she played her tambourine and led the singing that day.

Miriam had helped craft a plan to save her baby

brother's life. She had wondered if perhaps their miracle baby would grow up to deliver the Israelites from bondage in Egypt.

But then her hopes had been dashed when Moses was exiled for killing an Egyptian.

Imagine her surprise when years later her brother reappeared to lead the Israelites out of Egypt! When all hope was lost, Moses had shown up! God had indeed remembered His people and provided a way of escape. Miriam had a lot to celebrate!

What has God done in your life? Celebrate. Thank God for your salvation, and thank God specifically for a time He has shown up and restored your hope, just as He showed up for Miriam.

Pray:

Lord, make me one who celebrates Your goodness. Help me to take up my tambourine and sing out loud as Miriam did. May I never dismiss Your provision in my life as coincidence, but may I always recognize the ways You show up and provide for my needs. In Jesus' name I pray. Amen.

....

....

....

....

....

....

THE NAME OF THE LORD
Read Exodus 20:1–21

Key Verse:

"You shall not take the name of the LORD your God in vain, for the LORD will not hold him guiltless who takes His name in vain."
EXODUS 20:7 NKJV

Understand:

- *Do you take the Lord's name in vain? Why or why not?*

- *Are there ways that people take the Lord's name in vain without actually speaking His name?*

Apply:

It has become common in our culture to take God's name in vain. "Oh my—," followed by the Lord's name is a phrase that rolls off the tongues of our society's young children. Why? Because they hear it everywhere. The phrase is sprinkled into every movie and TV show. It is an exclamation spoken by adults all around them, often even their parents and teachers. And so they assume it must be okay. But is it?

God gave Moses Ten Commandments for the

people to follow. This was God's law. One of the Ten Commandments states clearly that we are not to take the Lord's name in vain.

Are you taking this command seriously? Are you honoring the name of your God? Do you use it when you are speaking to Him or sharing with others about His great glory? Or do you use it as a slang word, defaming your God each time it is spoken?

Pray:

Lord, I love You, and I will follow Your command to honor Your name, never mindlessly using it in vain. Please help me always to fear and respect You as the sovereign God of the universe. In this casual society, help me not to come before You casually but with the utmost respect. In Jesus' name I pray. Amen.

....

....

....

....

....

....

....

....

....

....

....

AVOID IDOLS
Read Leviticus 19:1–37

Key Verse:

Do not turn to idols or make metal gods for yourselves. I am the LORD your God.
LEVITICUS 19:4 NIV

Understand:

- *Among the laws laid out for the Israelites, we read that they were not to turn to idols. Why do you think this was, and is, so important to God?*

- *What is your definition of an idol?*

Apply:

While this law was given in Leviticus, it still applies to believers today. It is repeated in the New Testament, and we know that our God is a jealous God. In 1 Corinthians 10:14, the apostle Paul warns the believers in Corinth to keep away from idols.

Must an idol be fashioned from metal or wood? Do you think that the Lord is also jealous of other types of idols? An idol is anything that we put before God in our lives. Do you spend more time reading the Bible or on social media sites? Do you focus on prayer or TV more often?

Consider today where you're putting most of your time and money. You may find your idols lurking there. Make a conscious effort to turn away from such idols and seek God first and with your whole heart. This pleases the Lord.

Pray:

Heavenly Father, bring to light anything in my life that I have allowed to become an idol. I may not be constructing other gods of metal or wood, but I am distracted daily by my own idols. Create in me a pure heart that puts You first in all I do. Amen.

....

....

....

....

....

....

....

....

....

....

....

....

DON'T MISS YOUR PROMISED LAND

Read Numbers 14:1–25

Key Verse:

So not one of them will see the land I promised to their ancestors. No one who rejected me will see that land.
NUMBERS 14:23 NCV

Understand:

- *God had proven Himself faithful to the Israelites. Why do you think they struggled to believe He would protect them as they entered the Promised Land?*

- *What does this type of fear look like in your own life? What promises in scripture will you claim that can help ease your fears?*

Apply:

God had led the Israelites out of Egypt. He had promised them this land that was right before them. And yet what did they do? They refused to go in. They heard the report that there were giants in the land. They let their fear get the best of them. They turned against Moses and Aaron. They even concocted a plan to return to Egypt, where they had been enslaved.

This all seems really silly, and we can sit back and point our fingers at the Israelites until. . .we look closely at our own lives.

God has promised never to forsake us. He has promised us abundant and eternal life. He has assured us that He has a hope and a future for us and that He does not intend to bring us harm. And yet how many times do we shrink back in fear, forgetting that we are heirs of the King?

Pray:

Lord, I lay hold of Your promises today. I claim them one by one. I rest assured that You are in control and that You are sovereign. Help me to trust You more, I ask. I don't want to miss out on Your blessings for my life simply due to unnecessary fear. In Jesus' name I pray. Amen.

....

....

....

....

....

....

....

....

....

....

TEACHABLE MOMENTS
Read Deuteronomy 6:1–25

Key Verses:

"And these words which I command you today shall be in your heart. You shall teach them diligently to your children, and shall talk of them when you sit in your house, when you walk by the way, when you lie down, and when you rise up."
DEUTERONOMY 6:6–7 NKJV

Understand:

- *When were the Israelites commanded to speak of the Lord's words and to whom were they to teach these words diligently?*

- *When do you grasp teachable moments with your children?*

Apply:

So many teachable moments are packed into every day. The challenge is to lay hold of them and not let them pass by untapped. While the command here in Deuteronomy was for Israelite parents of that day, we know it is true for us today as well.

Had Deuteronomy been written today, perhaps this verse would read: *Teach them to your children diligently. Talk of them when you sit in your car driving back and forth to school and extracurricular activities. Teach them when you are going through the drive-through and waiting in line at the grocery store* . . . . You get the idea. Times have changed, but the Word of God remains the same yesterday, today, and tomorrow.

Grasp those teachable moments as you are walking and talking with your children. They need to know the Word of God, and they will only know if you teach them.

Pray:

Lord, I get so busy. I am guilty of putting a phone or tablet in my kids' hands far too often just to occupy them so I can find my sanity again. Please help me to use the teachable moments You give me each day with these children. Time passes so quickly, and I want them to know, love, and honor Your Word. Amen.

....

....

....

....

....

....

....

....

....

....

GOD GOES BEFORE YOU
Read Deuteronomy 31:1–30

Key Verse:

*"The L*ORD* himself will go before you. He will be with you; he will not leave you or forget you. Don't be afraid and don't worry."*
DEUTERONOMY 31:8 NCV

Understand:

- *What are the promises packed into the key verse for today?*

- *What challenge will you face less afraid knowing that the Lord goes before you?*

Apply:

Regardless of the fact that God had promised them the land of Canaan, the Israelites of the past had been too afraid to enter. They feared the giants who lived in this amazing land. After a period of forty years in the wilderness as God's punishment for their lack of faith, this new generation was ready to go in. It was critical that they hear the words of Moses or they too might forfeit the land that flowed with milk and honey.

They were not to fear. God was with them. He would not leave them or forget them. They were commanded not to worry.

Where are you hesitant? Where do you need to step out in faith? When we shrink back from taking a step of faith where God is clearly leading us, we forfeit amazing blessings. Claim these promises in your own life today. God is with you. He goes before you. He will not leave or forget you. Trust Him.

Pray:

Heavenly Father, I will go where You lead. Help me to lay down fear and worry. I want to trade those hindrances for Your help and Your faithfulness. I know that You go before me. Wherever You may lead, I will follow in faith. Amen.

....

....

....

....

....

....

....

....

....

....

....

STRONG AND COURAGEOUS

Read Joshua 1:1–18

Key Verses:

"This book of the law shall not depart from your mouth, but you shall meditate on it day and night, so that you may be careful to do according to all that is written in it; for then you will make your way prosperous, and then you will have success. Have I not commanded you? Be strong and courageous! Do not tremble or be dismayed, for the LORD your God is with you wherever you go."

JOSHUA 1:8–9 NASB

Understand:

- *What does it mean to meditate on the Word of God? How is meditating on it different from just reading it?*

- *We are commanded to be strong and courageous. How does this look in your workplace? How does it look when you are teased because of a choice you make because you are following God's Word?*

Apply:

Just as this promise was true for the Israelites who claimed the land God had given them, it is true for you today. God is for you. He is with you wherever you go.

Joshua 1:8 commands believers to meditate on scripture day and night so that we will be careful to do what is written in it. These are strong words of advice, and they are followed with strong words about reward. What does the passage say? If we do what the Bible says, we will be prosperous and successful.

If there is any verse in the Bible that inspires you to spend time in the Word of God, it's probably Joshua 1:8. And the verse that immediately follows promises you that God goes with you. Claim these promises, and remember to discipline yourself to follow what the Bible says in every situation.

Pray:

God, thank You for Your holy Word. These verses remind me how important it is that I do not just leave my Bible in the car after church on Sunday but that I spend time in it daily. Your Word is my pathway to success, and I want to honor You by doing what it says. In Jesus' name I pray. Amen.

....

....

....

....

....

....

....

A WOMAN OF REASON
Read Judges 13:1–25

Key Verses:

Manoah said, "We have seen God, so we will surely die." But his wife said to him, "If the LORD wanted to kill us, he would not have accepted our burnt offering or grain offering. He would not have shown us all these things or told us all this."
JUDGES 13:22–23 NCV

Understand:

- *Why should we, as Christians, avoid panicking or overreacting? What should we do instead?*

- *Manoah's wife was a support to her husband. How do you support your husband, if you are married? If you are single, how do you support other family members or friends?*

Apply:

Manoah and his wife could not have children. You can imagine her delight, then, when Manoah's wife was visited by the angel of the Lord and told she would become pregnant! She was told the boy would be a Nazarite, dedicated to God his entire life.

Later the couple watched the angel literally disappear, rising up with the flame from their burnt offering to the Lord. At this, they realized this truly was the angel of the Lord! Manoah overreacted and stated that they would surely die because they had seen God. But the reason of a woman came in handy at the time. Manoah's wife reminded him of the great news they had received. Why would God want them to die? He was giving them a son, and also, He had accepted their offering.

Their son Samson was soon born. Manoah's wife proved to be the voice of reason in her family. We should do likewise when our husbands or children are in a state of panic.

Pray:

Lord, help me not to be the one who panics and overreacts in my family. Use me as a source of calm and reason. I want to trust You in all things. Every day has enough worry of its own. Help me to walk in trust that You always have the best interest of my loved ones and myself in mind. Amen.

....

....

....

....

....

....

....

....

LOYALTY
Read Ruth 1:1–22

Key Verses:

But Ruth said, "Do not urge me to leave you or turn back from following you; for where you go, I will go, and where you lodge, I will lodge. Your people shall be my people, and your God, my God. Where you die, I will die, and there I will be buried. Thus may the LORD do to me, and worse, if anything but death parts you and me."
RUTH 1:16–17 NASB

Understand:

- *Why do you think Ruth refused to go back to her homeland?*

- *When Ruth chose Naomi's God, she chose to follow the one true God rather than the gods of her homeland. How did this change Ruth's life?*

Apply:

Naomi's husband and two sons died, and she was left in a foreign land, Moab, with her two daughters-in-law. She headed home to Bethlehem where she heard there was food. She told her two daughters-in-law to go back to their homes and their gods. She knew they must find new husbands because in that day, a woman needed a husband to provide for her. Orpah obeyed, but Ruth refused to leave her mother-in-law. She clung to Naomi, demonstrating a loyalty seldom found in today's world. She journeyed with Naomi to the land of Bethlehem.

As chapter 1 of Ruth closes, Ruth and Naomi have arrived in Bethlehem just in time for the barley harvest. This is how God works. His timing is perfect. God's plan to provide for Ruth and Naomi is a beautiful story as the book of Ruth continues to unfold. Ruth's faithfulness to her mother-in-law inspires us to be loyal, regardless of the cost.

Pray:

Help me, Lord, to be found loyal to my family and friends. May I be like Ruth who refused to turn away and leave her mother-in-law in need. May I be one who is found faithful to You and to those who are in need. Amen.

....

....

....

....

....

....

....

....

NAOMI'S BLESSING
Read Ruth 4:1–22

Key Verses:

Then Naomi took the child and laid him in her lap, and became his nurse. The neighbor women gave him a name, saying, "A son has been born to Naomi!" So they named him Obed. He is the father of Jesse, the father of David.
RUTH 4:16–17 NASB

Understand:

- *Have you ever experienced joy that was born from sorrow? In other words, a blessing that came after a very hard loss or disappointment?*

- *When God promises to use all things for good for those who love Him (see Romans 8:28), what do you think that means?*

Apply:

Naomi had experienced great sorrow, but God was not finished with her story. He led her back to Bethlehem and provided a loyal daughter-in-law, Ruth, to journey with her.

Ruth gathered barley in the fields of Boaz and caught his attention. He was touched by her loyalty to Naomi, and he showed her generosity. Boaz purchased the land that had belonged to Naomi's late husband in order to acquire Ruth and Naomi. He married Ruth and cared for both of the women.

Naomi was given a grandson through Ruth even though Ruth was not her biological daughter. She became nurse to little Obed. Obed would one day be the father of Jesse and the grandfather of King David, from whose line came the Messiah, Jesus.

God works in mysterious ways, but He always uses all things for good for those who love Him.

Pray:

Lord, even when I walk through the valley of the shadow of death, help me to remember that You are with me. You will use all things for good in my life because I love You. Amen.

....

....

....

....

....

....

....

....

....

A VOW KEPT
Read 1 Samuel 1:1–28

Key Verses:

"For this child I prayed, and the LORD has granted me my petition which I asked of Him. Therefore I also have lent him to the LORD; as long as he lives he shall be lent to the LORD." So they worshiped the LORD there.

1 SAMUEL 1:27–28 NKJV

Apply:

- *For what had Hannah prayed? What shows us in these verses that she had prayed fervently and over an extended period of time?*

- *What was her vow to the Lord, which she fulfilled when Samuel was born?*

Understand:

Hannah prayed to the Lord for a child. She didn't just pray now and then. No, she wept and prayed earnestly and often. She prayed so fervently in the presence of Eli that the priest thought she was drunk.

When Samuel was born, Hannah kept the vow that she had made. As soon as he was weaned, Hannah took him to Eli. She dedicated and gave Samuel to the Lord.

After God had granted Hannah's desire for a child, she could have forgotten her promise. Don't you imagine she longed to keep her beloved son with her and watch him grow? This is a story of earnest prayer that availed much, and a vow kept.

For what do you long? Do you pray earnestly for it? Is the prayer for something that can bring glory to God? Examine your own heart as you read the story of Hannah.

Heavenly Father, You know my deepest longings and desires. Mold my heart and mind so that I will think like You and desire only that which will bring You glory. Like Hannah did, help me to honor You with all the good gifts You bestow upon my life. Amen.

....

....

....

....

....

....

....

....

....

....

GOD SEES THE HEART
Read 1 Samuel 16:1–23

Key Verse:

But the LORD said to Samuel, "Do not look at his appearance or at his physical stature, because I have refused him. For the LORD does not see as man sees; for man looks at the outward appearance, but the LORD looks at the heart."
1 SAMUEL 16:7 NKJV

Understand:

- *What are some common methods that we as humans use for judging others? (e.g., by social class, by level of education, by race. . .)*

- *According to 1 Samuel 16:7, how does the Lord judge a person?*

Apply:

Young man after young man paraded before Samuel. Their father, Jesse, probably watched Samuel expectantly. Don't you imagine he looked for a sparkle in Samuel's eye or a nod of his head to indicate the son who would be chosen to serve as king? And yet Samuel said again and again, "This is not the one the Lord has chosen."

Jesse couldn't imagine that the chosen one could be the youngest, David, who was tending the sheep.

When young David stood before Samuel, the Lord pronounced him the chosen one. David was anointed with oil, and the Spirit of the Lord came upon him.

How do you see those around you? Or even yourself? Do you judge by the outward appearance or by the heart? God sees the heart.

Pray:

Help me, Lord, not to judge a book by its cover. While a person may do or say all the right things, it is his or heart that You see. The race, social status, and even personality of a person is not what You see. You see the heart. Help me to follow Your example in this. Amen.

....

....

....

....

....

....

....

....

....

....

CONFIDENCE IN GOD
Read 1 Samuel 17:1–58

Key Verse:

And David said, "The LORD who delivered me from the paw of the lion and from the paw of the bear, He will deliver me from the hand of this Philistine." And Saul said to David, "Go, and may the LORD be with you."
1 SAMUEL 17:37 NASB

Understand:

- *What gave David the confidence to fight Goliath, the Philistine giant?*

- *What experiences have you had that give you confidence to face an unknown future with a known God?*

Apply:

As a shepherd, David's job was to watch over the sheep. This job entailed fighting off wild animals that intended to kill the sheep. David had become skilled at his work. God had protected him. He had not died from a bear or lion attack, and for a shepherd, these were very real possibilities.

What David had faced in his past enabled him to face a new challenge with confidence. But notice this: It was not David's confidence in himself or in his own strength or ability that led him to fight the giant. It was his trust in the Lord.

"The LORD who delivered me. . ." was the one David bragged on, not himself.

Look back at your life. Where has God protected or delivered you? God will use each of your experiences to prepare you for the next. Be prepared for a greater challenge that lies ahead.

Pray:

Lord, thank You for the times You have protected me and provided a way of escape. You have built up in me a confidence that next time and the time after that, You will remain faithful. You will show up. Help me to trust in Your strength as You continue to use me and to put challenges in my path. Amen.

....

....

....

....

....

....

....

....

....

....

ABIGAIL'S WISDOM
Read 1 Samuel 25:1–44

Key Verses:

David answered Abigail, "Praise the LORD, the God of Israel, who sent you to meet me. May you be blessed for your wisdom. You have kept me from killing or punishing people today."
1 SAMUEL 25:32–33 NCV

Understand:

- *Has God ever given you wisdom that something needed to be done or said and it needed to happen quickly? What did you do?*

- *What do you think you would have done in Abigail's situation? Would you have been bold enough to go before David in such a manner?*

Apply:

Abigail is described in 1 Samuel 25 as beautiful and wise; her husband, Nabal, as cruel and mean. What a contrast!

As Nabal's wife, Abigail had a front-row seat to this man's drunkenness, selfishness, and anger. She knew, just as the servant said, that there was no sense trying to reason with Nabal.

Abigail acted quickly and wisely. She courageously approached David and reasoned with him in order to save her family and Nabal's men. She left Nabal to God.

What or whom do you need to leave to God? It's tempting to seek revenge or to wish harm upon people who mistreat us. When Abigail left her husband to God, he was turned to stone in a matter of days! Rest assured that the ungodly will see their demise.

We are called to live at peace as much as it is in our control and to walk humbly with our God. Leave evildoers in His hands, and use your time and talents as Abigail did—for good.

Pray:

Lord, give me the wisdom of Abigail. Help me to be a problem solver for Your Kingdom. Where wisdom is needed, I ask that You grant me a sound mind. When I need to take action, I pray that You will show me that as well. In Jesus' name I ask these things. Amen.

....

....

....

....

....

....

....

....

GOD WILL MAKE
ALL THINGS RIGHT
Read 2 Samuel 7:1–29

Key Verse:

*"Your house and your kingdom will endure forever before me;
your throne will be established forever."*
2 SAMUEL 7:16 NIV

Understand:

- *To whom does God reveal information about
  David in 2 Samuel 7?*

- *How does knowing that Jesus eventually
  comes from the line of David change the way
  you interpret God's promises to David in
  these verses?*

Apply:

In the Garden of Eden, man made a choice to turn away from God. This is known as the Fall. Because of the Fall, we have death in the world. There was no physical death prior to it. We also have shame. Adam and Eve clothed themselves with fig leaves to hide from the Lord after they had sinned against Him. As a result of the Fall, things are not right in the world. Things are not as God designed and desired.

When God put King David on the throne, a

promise was revealed. It was a promise that God was establishing a throne that would endure forever. How is that? Because Jesus Himself would come from the line of David.

Way back in 2 Samuel, God was working out a plan of restoration. Through Christ, we are reconciled with God. And one day God will once again make all things right in His world. Heaven will be even grander than Eden!

Pray:

Heavenly Father, I thank You that on my darkest day and when I face my deepest disappointment, I can remember that You have overcome this world. You are working out Your plans just as You were in 2 Samuel. One day You will make all things right again. Amen.

....

....

....

....

....

....

....

....

....

....

A WISE WOMAN
Read 2 Samuel 20:1–26

Key Verses:

Then the woman said, "In the past people would say, 'Ask for advice at Abel,' and the problem would be solved. I am one of the peaceful, loyal people of Israel. You are trying to destroy an important city of Israel. Why must you destroy what belongs to the LORD?"

2 SAMUEL 20:18–19 NCV

Understand:

- *Whose wise, godly counsel do you seek?*
- *Does anyone turn to you for such counsel?*

Apply:

Joab was ready to destroy an entire city in order to kill one bad seed, a man who had turned against King David. Instead of just standing by and letting this happen, a wise woman shouted out. She stood up for what was right. She stepped in and, in effect, saved the day!

Joab listened to the voice of wisdom. He heard the woman's reasoning. She asked him why he was going to destroy that which belonged to God. Why destroy the whole city instead of just killing the one man he was after? Joab agreed when the woman said they would toss the man's head over the wall to him!

These verses from 2 Samuel tell us that not only did the woman offer Joab wise counsel, but she also spoke wisely to all the people of the city. Are you bold enough to stand for what is right, to protect human life, and to offer wise counsel when it is needed?

Pray:

Lord, help me to know when to speak up and when to remain silent. There is a time for both, and it's often hard to discern the difference. Help me also to know who to go to when I need godly advice. In Jesus' name I ask. Amen.

....

....

....

....

....

....

....

....

....

....

....

....

CHOSEN
Read 2 Kings 2:1–22

Key Verse:

As they were walking and talking, a chariot and horses of fire appeared and separated Elijah from Elisha. Then Elijah went up to heaven in a whirlwind.
2 KINGS 2:11 NCV

Understand:

- *How did Elijah go to heaven?*
- *Who had remained very close to Elijah until he was taken up into heaven?*

Apply:

Elisha had refused to leave Elijah until the very end. He had stuck to him like glue, a faithful friend. Perhaps he wanted to see Elijah taken up into heaven to confirm and strengthen his own faith. Perhaps he just wanted to be with him as long as he possibly could. What we do know is that he remained faithful. He refused to leave Elijah's side.

When Elijah asked Elisha what he could do for him, the only desire Elisha expressed was to have a double portion of his spirit. He didn't want wealth or fame, only to be very well equipped to serve God.

Do you stand by and support your spiritual

mentors, those who are teaching and preaching the Gospel as Elisha supported Elijah? Do you stick closer than a brother? And what is your desire in doing so? Do you desire to learn as much as you can and to serve God in an even greater way?

Consider your loyalty and your motives. You will be blessed if they are pure before God.

Pray:

Lord, I do not understand the mystery as to why Elijah was lifted into heaven as he was. Make me as faithful as Elisha to the work of Your Kingdom. Help me not to desire any other thing than more of Your Spirit, greater ability to serve and love You better. Amen.

....

....

....

....

....

....

....

....

....

....

SIMPLE ACTS OF KINDNESS
Read 2 Kings 4:1–44

Key Verses:

The woman said to her husband, "I know that this is a holy man of God who passes by our house all the time. Let's make a small room on the roof and put a bed in the room for him. We can put a table, a chair, and a lampstand there. Then when he comes by, he can stay there."

2 KINGS 4:9–10 NCV

Understand:

- *Have you gone out of your way to show hospitality to someone?*

- *Has someone ever been particularly kind to you? How did it make you feel?*

Apply:

The Shunammite woman saw a need and wanted to meet it. She recognized that Elisha was a holy man of God. She proposed to her husband that rather than just feeding him a meal each time he passed their way, they should provide a room for him in their home. Isn't it kind how she planned the details? She decided that a table, chair, and lampstand in addition to the bed would go into the small room on the roof for Elisha.

This simple act of kindness and hospitality was not done for a reward. The woman did not ask for anything in return. But, amazingly, she was granted a son because of her gesture.

When you see a need that you are able to meet, meet it. The most basic act of kindness can make all the difference in someone's life. And God sees your good deeds. If not in this life, you will find your reward in heaven. The Lord is pleased when we serve and love one another.

Pray:

Lord, all of my resources come straight from Your hand. Nothing that I have—my home, my car, even the food in my pantry—belongs to me. It is all on loan from You. Please show me opportunities to use my resources to meet the needs of those around me. Make me hospitable and kind like the Shunammite woman. In Christ's name I pray. Amen.

....

....

....

....

....

....

....

....

....

FOR SUCH A TIME AS THIS
Read Esther 4:1–17

Key Verse:

"If you keep quiet at this time, someone else will help and save the Jewish people, but you and your father's family will all die. And who knows, you may have been chosen queen for just such a time as this."
ESTHER 4:14 NCV

Understand:

- *How might God desire to use you in your current circumstances?*

- *Are you willing to take risks for the kingdom of God?*

Apply:

The story of Esther reminds us of God's sovereignty. Through a series of events, Esther, a Jewish orphan, became a queen of Persia. When the time was right, God motioned Esther onto the stage and used her in a starring role to save the Israelite people.

God has orchestrated your life in a similar manner. Consider the circumstances God has used to bring you to this place in life. Do you have a platform you can use for furthering God's kingdom? Do you have authority that enables you to make decisions that honor Him? Perhaps you can look to your left and your right and see others who need to know the Savior.

You are where you are "for just such a time as this." Be a modern-day Esther. Take a risk as she did when she went before the king. There is great reward in knowing you are in the center of God's will.

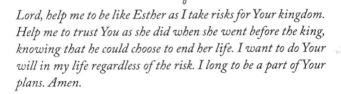

Pray:

Lord, help me to be like Esther as I take risks for Your kingdom. Help me to trust You as she did when she went before the king, knowing that he could choose to end her life. I want to do Your will in my life regardless of the risk. I long to be a part of Your plans. Amen.

....

....

....

....

....

....

....

....

....

....

STAND OUT AS A BELIEVER
Read Psalms 1:1–2:12

Key Verses:

Blessed is the one
  who does not walk in step with the wicked
or stand in the way that sinners take
  or sit in the company of mockers,
but whose delight is in the law of the LORD,
  and who meditates on his law day and night.
PSALM 1:1–2 NIV

Understand:

- *What is the difference between walking in step with sinners and standing in the way that sinners take?*

- *How and when do you meditate on God's Word? If this is not a regular practice for you, how and when will you begin?*

Apply:

Believers are called to be different. We are to stand out. We are not to look like the world, walk in step with the world, or even get near the road of sin that leads to destruction.

When the jokes become coarse, do you laugh with everyone else? After all, you weren't the one who told the joke. You're just joining in with an innocent giggle.

When gossip is presented to you, do you turn toward it for another juicy morsel or do you turn away from it, making it clear that you're not interested?

Each day, the believer has opportunities to stand firm and to stand out. Be different. Don't blend in with the crowd.

Be like the tree planted by streams of water. Yield your fruit. Your leaf will never wither. Claim the promise of the One who walks with God.

Lord, make me strong. Give me the boldness to stand for what is right when I am tempted to go in the way of sin. Help me to dwell on Your Word day and night that it might strengthen me. In Jesus' name I pray. Amen.

....

....

....

....

....

....

....

....

WAIT ON THE LORD

Read Psalms 27:1–28:9

Key Verse:

Wait for the Lord;
Be strong and let your heart take courage;
Yes, wait for the Lord.
Psalm 27:14 NASB

Understand:

- *Strength and courage are mentioned in Psalm 27:14. What are you waiting for currently that requires strength and courage?*

- *We are called to wait for the Lord. His timing is perfect. Where have you seen this in your own life?*

Apply:

The psalmist cries out to God in Psalm 27. He declares God as his light, his salvation, his help, the lifter of his head, and his defense. He calls him Lord. He says that even his own mother and father have left him but that God continues to be faithful. He has received protection from God. He then admonishes us to be strong and courageous and wait for the Lord.

You may be in a desert place right now. You may

not feel that God "has your back," but He does. He is working out His will for you even when you cannot sense it. Trust in the dark what you have seen in the light. There will come a day when you will look back and see how God was with you even in the hardest times.

Wait on the Lord. He is near.

Pray:

Lord, when I do not feel You near, remind me that You promise never to leave or forsake me. You are my protector and provider. I will praise You all the days of my life. Help me to wait well when I am required to do so. In Jesus' name I pray. Amen.

....

....

....

....

....

....

....

....

....

....

....

CALL UPON THE LORD
Read Psalms 86:1–87:7

Key Verses:

Give ear, O LORD, to my prayer;
And attend to the voice of my supplications.
In the day of my trouble I will call upon You,
For You will answer me.
PSALM 86:6–7 NKJV

Understand:

- *When you run into trouble, who do you call on first? A friend? A family member?*

- *The psalmist states that he will call on the Lord in his day of trouble. Why? What will the result most certainly be according to today's key verses?*

Apply:

You know the type of day. Everything goes wrong. Just when you thought you were breaking even financially, your hot water heater goes out. Or your property taxes go up drastically. Or the school is asking for more money for extracurricular activities. On top of that, no one in the family can seem to get along. Everyone is bickering. There is eye rolling, and the blame game is nonstop. Tattling and arguing are also abundant. You want to yell out, as the lady in the bubble bath commercial, "Calgon, take me away!"

When you have one of "those" days, who do you tend to call first? Many women tend to pick up the phone to call a girlfriend, mom, or sister. Next time you are struggling, instead of heading for your cell phone, call on your heavenly Father. God is always there, and He cares. He wants you to turn to Him. He will answer.

Pray:

Lord, rather than dumping my troubles on my husband or mom, I will choose to call on Your mighty name. My girlfriends and sisters can only do so much, but You are the sovereign God of the universe. You are big enough to handle even my very worst day. Thank You for hearing my prayers and answering when I am in trouble. Amen.

....

....

....

....

....

....

....

....

SECURE IN CHRIST
Read Psalms 91:1–92:15

Key Verses:

"Because he loves me," says the LORD, "I will rescue him;
I will protect him, for he acknowledges my name.
He will call on me, and I will answer him;
I will be with him in trouble,
I will deliver him and honor him.
With long life I will satisfy him
and show him my salvation."
PSALM 91:14–16 NIV

Understand:

- *Make a list of all the actions God promises to take in Psalm 91. Which ones stand out to you as especially comforting?*

- *When does God promise to answer prayer in Psalm 91:15?*

Apply:

It is often said that a man's greatest need is respect and a woman's greatest need is security. Would you agree that you long to feel secure? Most women would answer with a resounding "yes!"

The good news is that whether or not you have a husband, you have a God who is all about protecting you. Under the shadow of His wing, you are safe (see Psalm 36:7).

Psalm 91 is full of strong verbs because they describe your even stronger God. Words like *rescue, save, cover, guard, protect,* and *deliver*—just to name a few—help us to get a clear picture of the security we have in God. He is better than the strongest bodyguard or bouncer on earth!

Psalm 92 describes the righteous as glad, exalted, flourishing, and bearing fruit. If you trust in the Lord for your security, you will never be disappointed. And in the end, you will blossom into the confident woman He so desires you to become.

Pray:

Help me, Father, to ultimately depend on You for my security. Thank You for Your constant protection. Lead me in Your ways, and help me to revere You and to live in the shadow of Your wings, secure in my faith. Amen.

....

....

....

....

....

....

....

....

GOD'S ECONOMY

Read Psalms 113:1–114:8

Key Verses:

He raises the poor from the dust
And lifts the needy from the ash heap,
To make them sit with princes,
With the princes of His people.
PSALM 113:7–8 NASB

Understand:

- *How did Jesus humble himself when He came to earth? Why did He do this?*

- *God often chooses the lowly over those with wealth or power. Name some examples of this from the Bible.*

Apply:

In this world, often those with power or money appear to end up on top. They drive the fancy cars, have the best jobs, and experience all the luxuries this life has to offer. In God's economy, things are quite different. He often chooses to exalt the humble.

God chose a prostitute named Rahab to provide protection for some of His men. He even sent His own Son to earth to be born in a manger and to be raised in the home of Joseph, a carpenter. Jesus called fishermen as His closest disciples, those who "did life" with him throughout His earthly ministry!

Praise God today for being God. There is no other like Him, as Psalm 113 declares. Thank Him for seeing the hearts of men and women rather than just the exterior. Remember to see others as God sees them. They are precious in His sight regardless of their status or state.

Pray:

Lord, You are able to turn things around in our lives. Psalm 113 says that You give barren women children. You seat the poor at Your table as guests. Thank You for loving us so. Amen.

....

....

....

....

....

....

....

....

....

....

....

WAITING WELL
Read Psalms 130:1–132:18

Key Verse:

I wait for the LORD, my whole being waits, and in his word I put my hope.
PSALM 130:5 NIV

Understand:

- *Have you ever had to wait a long time for something? How did it feel?*

- *What do you think it looks like to put your hope in God's Word as you wait?*

Apply:

Many times in life we are called on to wait. We wait in lines at movie theaters and grocery stores. We wait for Christmas and birthdays. As humans, we certainly know about waiting. What kind of waiter are you? Do you grumble or lose faith? Or do you patiently put your trust in God?

The psalmist says that his whole being waits for the Lord. When we rest before God with every part of our being, He meets us right there where we are. Seek to rest mentally, emotionally, physically, and spiritually before God. He is your Abba Father, your Daddy. He has your best interest at heart, and He is never early or late but always right on time.

Wait on the Lord, and claim the promises He has given you in His Word. He has not forgotten you. He will never leave you. He is your Good Shepherd. He will see you through, and the waiting will be worth it in the end.

Pray:

Lord, as I wait, please help me to know that Your timing is always right for me. You always have my best interest at heart. In the waiting, help me to claim Your promises and to trust in Your Word. Amen.

....

....

....

....

....

....

....

....

....

....

....

....

A WISE MOTHER
Read Proverbs 1:1–33

Key Verses:

My child, listen when your father corrects you.
Don't neglect your mother's instruction.
What you learn from them will crown you with grace
and be a chain of honor around your neck.

PROVERBS 1:8–9 NLT

Understand:

- *What do the first seven verses of Proverbs 1 state that the proverbs are intended for?*

- *If you are a mother, are you teaching and correcting your children in such a manner that grace and honor will be their reward if they heed your words?*

Apply:

What are you teaching your children? Do you correct them when their behavior or attitudes are not godly? If you do, be encouraged. You are the type of mother who is spoken of in Proverbs 1:8–9.

As a parent, you have an obligation to grasp teachable moments with your children. You are responsible for teaching them God's ways. You are also held accountable for correcting them and disciplining them as necessary.

Too many mothers these days let their children rule the roost. This is not of God. Be certain that as you are training and disciplining your children, you are thinking of their future. What will serve them best—to be coddled or to be taught? To be allowed utter freedom or to learn self-restraint? Be sure that you are mothering your children in God's way.

Godly parenting will pay off. Proverbs says your children will receive grace and honor as rewards for following your instructions.

Pray:

Help me, Lord, to be a mother who corrects and trains my children. Where I have been lazy, give me a renewed focus. Where I have allowed too much freedom, remind me that my children long for boundaries. I want to be a godly mother whose children will benefit from my teaching. Amen.

....

....

....

....

....

....

....

....

BUILDING YOUR HOME
Read Proverbs 14:1–45

Key Verse:

The wise woman builds her house,
But the foolish tears it down with her own hands.
PROVERBS 14:1 NASB

Understand:

- *Proverbs 14 provides a contrast between two types of individuals. What are they?*

- *What are the verbs, or action words, in Proverbs 14:1? Consider the meaning of each. Which one do you spend most of your time doing?*

Apply:

The home is a haven for a family. It's a place of peace where a family seeks refuge from the world. Some women get this right and some don't.

More often than not, the woman of the house sets the tone for the home. Are you setting a tone of peace or of strife? How do you greet your husband and children at the end of a long day? Do you instantly launch into a to-do list? Do you scold? Or do you provide warmth, nurturing, and acceptance?

The wise woman seeks to meet the needs of

her family. She is conscientious with finances. She encourages and builds up her husband and kids. She manages things rather than just letting them go. A home should not be a place of disorder and disarray.

Seek to honor God by being a builder rather than a destroyer of your home.

Pray:

Lord, forgive me for the times when I have forgotten the importance of my role. I want to be categorized as a wise woman and not as one who tears down her own home. Help me to be a student of my husband and children, learning them well, that I might know the ways to build them up and encourage them best. Amen.

....

....

....

....

....

....

....

....

....

....

ARE YOU ARGUMENTATIVE OR PEACEFUL?
Read Proverbs 27:1–27

Key Verses:

A continual dripping on a very rainy day
And a contentious woman are alike;
Whoever restrains her restrains the wind,
And grasps oil with his right hand.
PROVERBS 27:15–16 NKJV

Understand:

- *Would your husband (or others close to you) describe you as peaceful or argumentative?*

- *Is it easy to restrain the wind or grasp oil with one's hand? Consider the meaning of these verses. Is it even possible to do so? How does this impact your attitude about being quarrelsome?*

Apply:

Proverbs gives advice for having a God-centered life. The key verses today point us toward understanding the seriousness of the contentious wife. The New Contemporary Version uses the word *quarreling* in place of *contentious.*

What is the first thing you say to your husband

each morning? The last thing you discuss at night? Are you affirming him for a hard day's work or pestering him about the chores that remain undone? Do you greet him with a hug and kiss, or with a list of complaints?

Take note of this proverb's warning. No man wants to make his home with a contentious woman. Trying to change this trait in a woman is like attempting to hold back the wind or hold oil in one's bare hand. Next time you start to pick a fight, hold your tongue. Find a way to praise your husband instead. See what a difference this makes in your marriage.

Pray:

Lord, I have not meant to be argumentative, but I do find myself dwelling on the negative lately. Help me to focus on my husband's strengths and be a wife who is supportive and loving. Look deep into my heart, and help me to root out any contentiousness that lives there. Amen.

....

....

....

....

....

....

....

A PROVERBS 31 WOMAN
Read Proverbs 31:1–30

Key Verse:

Charm can fool you, and beauty can trick you,
but a woman who respects the LORD should be praised.
PROVERBS 31:30 NCV

Understand:

- *What traits impress you in your female friends?*

- *As you read the chapter, underline or highlight traits of this godly woman who is described in Proverbs 31. Which of these traits do you possess? Which do you plan to work on developing?*

Apply:

The Proverbs 31 woman can overwhelm us if we let her! It's hard to compare to this amazing example. But this passage gives us a picture of a godly woman, wife, and mother. We can all learn from these words that admonish us to get up each day striving to be godly in all that we do.

Are you a Proverbs 31 woman? You may not be inspecting your fields or making linen cloth. But do you support your family in every way possible? Are you procrastinating and idle, or do you get up early to make sure things are ready for your family's day? There is much to be learned in Proverbs 31.

Verse 30 reminds us that outward beauty is only temporary. But the writer points out that the woman who fears the Lord is to be praised. The woman who has her priorities straight, as we read throughout this chapter, is to be honored and respected.

Pray:

God, help me to be a Proverbs 31 woman. I want to be a trustworthy wife and an honorable mother who sees to the needs of my family. Give me endurance when I am tired. Give me an extra dose of selflessness as it is needed. In Jesus' name I pray. Amen.

....

....

....

....

....

....

....

....

....

....

....

A TIME FOR EVERYTHING
Read Ecclesiastes 3:1–22

Key Verse:

To everything there is a season,
A time for every purpose under heaven.
ECCLESIASTES 3:1 NKJV

Understand:

- *Which of the verses in Ecclesiastes 3 have you experienced (e.g., a time to mourn)? Are there any that you have not yet experienced?*

- *What does it mean that God is sovereign? How is His sovereignty seen in this chapter?*

Apply:

Have you experienced some of the times mentioned in Ecclesiastes 3?

When a child dies, that is a time to mourn. It is also a time to be silent—simply out of an understanding that there are no words for such a loss. That is the time to be there for the family but not the time to try to fix their grief with words. The less spoken, the better.

There is also a time to rejoice. Have you rejoiced at baptisms, weddings, and other special events? Certainly, these call for celebration.

There are times to weep and times to laugh. Thank God that sorrow comes in waves. Just as the mighty ocean tosses us a strong breaker and we lose our balance, there comes a period of calm when we maintain our footing once again.

Accept the sovereignty of God. Accept the changes that life will throw your way. There is a time for everything.

Pray:

Heavenly Father, help me to know how to react to change in my life. Guide me as I seek to find the balance between laughter and sorrow, rejoicing and mourning. Life is an adventure. Thank You for being with me in every time and in every season. Amen.

....

....

....

....

....

....

....

....

....

....

GOD'S STRENGTH
Read Isaiah 40:1–41

Key Verse:

He gives power to the weak and strength to the powerless.
ISAIAH 40:29 NLT

Understand:

- *Isaiah 40 makes many statements about God. Which one grabs your attention? Why?*

- *What in this fallen world regularly drains you of strength and power?*

Apply:

The prophet Isaiah asks the reader to consider who can be compared to God. He reminds us that God places the stars in the sky and knows them by name. He points out the greatness of God, saying that all the nations are like a grain of sand in God's hand.

In today's key verse, we see that power and strength are gifts from God. God, who is full of power, gifts His children with power. He is the Source. We need only to tap into that Source in order to be filled with strength.

What drains you? Is it work? A dysfunctional relationship? Caring for your family? Old wounds that never seem to fully heal? Whatever zaps you of your strength, lay it down and ask God to fill you with power. He longs to see you thriving again! Just as the children's song says: "I am weak, but He is strong. Yes, Jesus loves me."

Pray:

Jesus, I am weak but You are strong. You are powerful, and I need some of that power to make it through the day. Bless me, I pray. Fill me with strength to face this fallen world with confidence and grit. I need You every hour! Thank You for the power source that You are to my life. Amen.

....

....

....

....

....

....

....

....

....

....

....

....

THE LORD IS WITH YOU

Read Isaiah 41:1–29

Key Verse:

"Do not fear, for I am with you;
Do not anxiously look about you, for I am your God.
I will strengthen you, surely I will help you,
Surely I will uphold you with My righteous right hand."
ISAIAH 41:10 NASB

Understand:

- *What does "looking anxiously about you" look like in your own life during times of trouble? Who are you tempted to turn to before you turn to God?*

- *What are God's promises in this one verse?*

Apply:

What are God's promises in this one verse? Break it down. He promises that He is with you. He says He is your God. He says He will strengthen you and help you. He promises to uphold you with His righteous right hand. That is a lot of promises for one verse of scripture!

While these promises were originally for an Israelite audience, they are true for all believers, and we can find great comfort in them.

What does God ask of you in this verse? He tells you not to fear and not to look about anxiously. That is a tall order, isn't it? When times of trouble come, it is our human reaction to pick up the phone and call a close friend or relative. Resist this urge. Look first and foremost to your God who promises to be with you and to help you. Take your fears and worries to Him. He is big enough to handle them all.

Pray:

Lord, I know that You are with me. Sometimes I look about anxiously, calling on everyone but You. Remind me to seek You first when I am in need. You stand ready to help me. What a blessing! Amen.

....

....

....

....

....

....

....

....

....

....

A NEW NAME
Read Isaiah 61:1–62:12

Key Verse:

You shall no longer be termed Forsaken,
Nor shall your land any more be termed Desolate;
But you shall be called Hephzibah, and your land Beulah;
For the LORD delights in you,
And your land shall be married.
ISAIAH 62:4 NKJV

Understand:

- *Are there names that you have given to*
  yourself or that you feel others have labeled
  you with?

- *Is it time to lay down some of those labels and*
  see yourself as God sees you?

Apply:

God's people had been in exile for years. He looked
at Israel and declared that they would have a new
name. He said that their new name would mean that
He delighted in His people. He would unite with
His people as a bridegroom chooses to unite with
his bride.

What name have you been going by for far too
long? Do you, like Israel, feel forsaken? Desolate?

Do you feel unworthy? Have you been labeled by yourself or others as a failure?

What name do you need to exchange for a new name today? God does not call you these names. God takes great delight in you. He created you, and He longs to enjoy fellowship with you. You are His daughter. You are, as a believer, given a new name. Refuse to cling to the past. Open your eyes to the bright future He has in store for you.

Pray:

Lord, I am tired of the old names. I have heard them ringing in my ears for too long now. I want to go by a new name. I want to see myself as You see me. Help me, Father, to remember that I am made in Your image and that You take delight in me. Amen.

....

....

....

....

....

....

....

....

....

DRAWING BOUNDARIES
Read Daniel 1:1–21

Key Verse:

God made Ashpenaz, the chief officer, want to be kind and merciful to Daniel.
DANIEL 1:9 NCV

Understand:

- *What did Daniel ask Ashpenaz for in Daniel 1? How did God show favor to Daniel in this request?*

- *In your own life, what boundary have you drawn because you are set apart as a child of God?*

Apply:

Daniel did not want to eat the food or drink the wine of the king of Babylon because it would make him unclean. He asked permission to abstain, and he found favor with the king's chief officer in this request.

Like young Daniel, an Israelite living in the Babylonian kingdom, you live in a society that is opposed to God's ways. What boundary have you drawn because you are a child of the living God? Have you drawn a boundary regarding modesty in your dress, what movies you watch, or your alcohol consumption? Maybe there is something else that you have drawn a line in the sand regarding.

God caused Daniel to find favor with the chief officer. As you seek to honor God, He will put people and circumstances in place to bless you. Trust Him, and keep living according to His ways despite opposition from those around you.

Pray:

Lord, thank You for the wonderful example of Daniel in the Bible. His story inspires me to draw boundaries and live according to Your will and Your ways in spite of the culture that is all around me. Give me strength to honor You with my decisions. In Jesus' name I ask. Amen.

....

....

....

....

....

....

....

....

....

....

TRUE REPENTANCE
Read Joel 2:1–32

Key Verse:

Rend your heart
  and not your garments.
Return to the LORD your God,
  for he is gracious and compassionate,
slow to anger and abounding in love,
  and he relents from sending calamity.
JOEL 2:13 NIV

Understand:

- *Have you ever truly felt brokenhearted over your own sin?*

- *In Joel 2:13, what adjectives are used to describe God's reaction to one who returns to Him? In other words, to one who repents of sin*

Apply:

How easy it is for us to stand in judgment of the Israelites as we read the stories of how quickly they forgot God's blessings. But we do the same, do we not?

When you sin, God is watching your reaction to that sin. He knows you will fall. We are living in a fallen world. But do you try to hide your sin? Do you diminish it, thinking to yourself, *Well, compared to this other person, I am not much of a sinner at all?*

Sin should break our hearts. God desires to see more than an outward expression of this brokenness. At the time of Joel, the people tore their clothing to express sorrow over sin. True repentance involves an inner sorrow, a tearing of the heart. God is quick to forgive when we come before Him broken and sorry for our sin.

Pray:

God, examine my heart. Show me if there is any attitude about my sin that displeases You. If I am quick to dismiss it as "not so bad," humble me. Remind me that You are holy and that sin is sin. Break my heart over my sin that I might truly repent and know Your gracious compassion in my life. Amen.

....

....

....

....

....

....

....

....

....

FOLLOWING GOD'S CALL
Read Jonah 1:1–2:10

Key Verses:

Now the LORD provided a huge fish to swallow Jonah, and Jonah was in the belly of the fish three days and three nights.
JONAH 1:17 NIV

From inside the fish Jonah prayed to the LORD his God. He said:
"In my distress I called to the LORD,
 and he answered me.
From deep in the realm of the dead I called for help,
 and you listened to my cry."
JONAH 2:1–2 NIV

Understand:

- *Why did Jonah end up in the belly of a great fish?*

- *Have you ever turned away and tried to hide from something you felt God calling you to do? How did it turn out?*

Apply:

Jonah avoided God's clear call to Nineveh because he knew God would graciously forgive the Assyrians in Nineveh. Jonah did not think they deserved God's mercy. He fled to a faraway land to hide from God.

Just as his predecessors' attempt to hide from God in the Garden of Eden, Jonah's attempt was unsuccessful. God was with him everywhere he went. He never lost sight of Jonah.

The Lord provided the large fish to swallow Jonah to save his life when the sailors cast him overboard. It was not just a physical lifesaving that Jonah received. His heart was changed in the belly of that fish. He reached rock bottom, and he cried out to God.

The next time you clearly sense God calling you to do something, do it. Learn from Jonah. Jonah thought he knew better than God, but God, in His sovereignty, always has a reason for what He asks of His children.

Pray:

God, I am thankful Jonah followed Your directions in the end. Many came to know You as a result. Help me to trust that while it may not be clear to me in the moment, You know the plans and my job is simply to obey. Make me ever sensitive to Your voice that I might hear Your call on my life. Amen.

....

....

....

....

....

....

SOVEREIGN GOD
Read Micah 5:1–6:8

Key Verse:

"But you, Bethlehem Ephrathah,
though you are small among the clans of Judah,
out of you will come for me
one who will be ruler over Israel,
whose origins are from of old,
from ancient times."
MICAH 5:2 NIV

Understand:

- *Micah prophesies about a ruler who will come from Bethlehem. Who is this ruler?*

- *When you read Old Testament verses that predict the coming of the Messiah, what do you think? How does it impact you?*

Apply:

Have you sung the old Christmas carol "O Little Town of Bethlehem"? The prophet Micah prophesied many years before the birth of Christ that a ruler would come from the little town of Bethlehem!

Isn't it amazing that prophets foretold the coming of Christ? God had a plan to redeem mankind all along. At just the right time, God sent His Son to redeem us (see Galatians 4:4–5).

Rest in the knowledge that you serve a great big God. If He is wise enough to craft a plan to save us from sin, is He not able to handle the hurts and hang-ups in your life? Turn to Him, acknowledge His presence, and leave your worries at the feet of a sovereign King.

Pray:

Lord, help me to trust in Your sovereignty. You are a great Creator. You reign over the universe. You set the stars in their places and call them by name. Surely You are able to manage my little life. I love You. Help me through this day to rely on You in every moment. Amen.

....

....

....

....

....

....

....

....

....

....

GOD SINGS OVER YOU

Read Zephaniah 3:1–20

Key Verse:

"The LORD your God is with you;
the mighty One will save you.
He will rejoice over you.
You will rest in his love;
he will sing and be joyful about you."
ZEPHANIAH 3:17 NCV

Understand:

- *What are the promises found in Zephaniah 3:17? Name each one.*

- *Which one are you in the deepest need of today?*

Apply:

While this promise was originally for the Israelites, we know that these promises ring true for us today as well. God has saved you if you have put your faith in Christ (see Acts 4:12). You can rest in His unconditional love (see Matthew 11:28–30).

Does it bring you comfort today to know that as you rest in the Lord, He sings over you and takes great delight in you? Have you ever rocked one of your children to sleep, singing over him or her until those little eyelids just cannot remain open? There is nothing more peaceful and delightful than watching your child rest. This is how God feels about you!

Rest in the Lord. Take refuge from the busyness and difficulty of the world. Find peace in His arms, and allow your heavenly Father to sing over you until things seem a bit more manageable.

Pray:

Lord, hearing that You sing over me makes You seem very close rather than far away. I know that You desire for me to find my rest in You. Help me to trust You enough to relinquish even my deepest fears and sorrows to Your more than capable hands. In Jesus' name I pray. Amen.

....

....

....

....

....

....

....

....

....

....

GIVING
Read Malachi 3:1–18

Key Verse:

"Bring the whole tithe into the storehouse, that there may be food in my house. Test me in this," says the LORD Almighty, "and see if I will not throw open the floodgates of heaven and pour out so much blessing that there will not be room enough to store it."
MALACHI 3:10 NIV

Understand:

- *What is God's promise here in relation to tithing?*

- *Do you currently give 10 percent of all that you earn to the Lord? If not, do these verses motivate you to begin giving regularly to the work of the Lord?*

Apply:

What is the first check you write after payday? Whether it's the beginning of each month or at the end of each two weeks, you probably have a regular day that you receive payment for your work. One of the greatest habits a Christian can form is that of giving back to the Lord. After all, everything we have comes from Him in the first place!

First Corinthians 16:2 points out that believers should give regularly, individually, and in proportion with our income. Many believers give 10 percent. Others start with this and increase their giving. The exact amount that you give to the Lord is personal, between you and God. What matters is that you give not out of duty but cheerfully (see 2 Corinthians 9:6–7). The Bible promises that those who give generously are, in turn, blessed. This is a promise you can "take to the bank"!

Pray:

Lord, I am so blessed to have the opportunity to give back to Your kingdom work. Allow me always to see giving and tithing as a blessing and never as a burden. In Jesus' name I pray. Amen.

....

....

....

....

....

....

....

....

....

LET YOUR LIGHT SHINE

Read Matthew 5:1–48

Key Verse:

"Let your light shine before men in such a way that they may see your good works, and glorify your Father who is in heaven."
MATTHEW 5:16 NASB

Understand:

- *Which blessing from the Beatitudes can you relate to? Why does it touch you most deeply?*

- *Why are we to let our light shine before men, according to Matthew 5:16?*

Apply:

There is a children's song sung in many churches that goes like this: "This little light of mine, I'm gonna let it shine.... Let it shine till Jesus comes.... I'm gonna let it shine."

But what does it mean to let your light shine?

It means you are called, as a Christ follower, to live differently. Your speech should set you apart. Your attitude should distinguish you from others. You should seem almost like an alien living on this earth because, in fact, that is what you are. This is not your home. Your home is in heaven with your Father.

Your good deeds are not to bring glory to

yourself but rather to illuminate the path that leads to your Father. When others ask you why you live as you do, point them to God. Let your light shine so that people will come to know Him.

Pray:

Lord, give me opportunities today to let my light shine brightly for You. Help me to be bold in my actions and with my words so that others may come to salvation through Christ. Amen.

....

....

....

....

....

....

....

....

....

....

....

....

....

....

YOUR FATHER SEES
Read Matthew 6:1–34

Key Verses:

"But when you do a charitable deed, do not let your left hand know what your right hand is doing, that your charitable deed may be in secret; and your Father who sees in secret will Himself reward you openly."
MATTHEW 6:3–4 NKJV

Understand:

- *What are some charitable deeds you have done recently or thought about doing?*

- *Why do you think it is important to God that believers do charitable deeds in secret?*

Apply:

Have you ever received an anonymous gift? Perhaps it was something small like a candy bar you found on your desk or in your mailbox at the office with no note attached. Maybe it was a larger gift, such as a debt that was paid off by an unknown hero. How did it make you feel?

God wants His children to give generously. His favorite type of giver is a cheerful one (see 2 Corinthians 9:7). And He sees when we go about giving in a quiet manner. God doesn't want us to get the glory for our gift. Instead, through our quiet or anonymous giving, He receives the glory!

Give God all the glory today. Perform a random act of kindness and smile as you walk away, knowing that you are not looking for man's praise but a reward that comes only from your Father in heaven.

Pray:

Lord, help me to be one who performs charitable deeds not for the glory of man but to bring You glory. I will seek not the reward of those around me but the reward that comes only from You. Amen.

....

....

....

....

....

....

....

....

....

....

....

....

DO NOT JUDGE
Read Matthew 7:1–29

Key Verses:

"Why do you look at the speck that is in your brother's eye, but do not notice the log that is in your own eye? Or how can you say to your brother, 'Let me take the speck out of your eye,' and behold, the log is in your own eye? You hypocrite, first take the log out of your own eye, and then you will see clearly to take the speck out of your brother's eye."

MATTHEW 7:3–5 NASB

Understand:

- *Are you ever tempted to judge someone before you know the person?*

- *Why is this dangerous?*

Apply:

Sometimes a child will tattle on another child to make himself or herself look better. This is not just a childish act. Unfortunately, we as adults often put others down in order to build up ourselves. It's easier to focus on another's fault than on our own.

Have you ever made the mistake of passing judgment on someone and later realized that you were wrong? Isn't it easy to look at the divorced woman and wonder what she did to ruin her marriage? Have you ever judged parents at the grocery store or in a restaurant for letting their children run wild?

God is love, and He wants us to love one another. We are not to gossip or slander or pass judgment on one another. That is not God's way. The next time you are tempted to judge someone else, consider this: *What challenges might that person have faced that you have been spared?* It will change the way you see others.

God, help me to see people as You do. Help me to see their hurts and wounds and not just their actions. So often I am quick to judge before I know the whole story. Give me grace and compassion and a loving heart that I might honor You in the way I view others. Show me where I can be an agent of Your love today. Amen.

....

....

....

....

....

....

....

....

....

SHARE JESUS:
STEP OUTSIDE THE BOX
Read Matthew 9:1–38

Key Verses:

As Jesus was having dinner at Matthew's house, many tax collectors and "sinners" came and ate with Jesus and his followers. When the Pharisees saw this, they asked Jesus' followers, "Why does your teacher eat with tax collectors and sinners?"

MATTHEW 9:10–11 NCV

Understand:

- *What is Jesus' answer to the question posed in Matthew 9:11? Read Matthew 9:12.*

- *Who are the tax collectors of today? Who would your friends be surprised to see you associating with?*

Apply:

We are called to live in this world. While we are set apart as believers, we are still to be "in the mix." If we isolate ourselves and associate only with one another, how will others come to know the healing salvation of Jesus Christ?

In these verses, the Pharisees are shocked to see Jesus eating and spending time with those they considered to be "sinners." In fact, we are all sinners. These tax collectors needed Christ. They needed rescue from a selfish and sinful life. Jesus stated that healthy people do not need physicians, but rather those who are sick need physicians. He gave wonderful analogies, and this one fits so well here.

Just as Jesus walked and talked with those who were the outcasts of society, those everyone knew to be sinners, we are to go and do likewise. Who in your community needs Jesus? Step outside the box. Jesus did.

Pray:

Lord, help me not to isolate myself among only other believers. While I know I must choose close friends who are Christians so that I can remain encouraged and strengthened, I also know I must not hide away. Give me opportunities to get out into my community and share Your love with those who need to know You. Amen.

LIGHTEN YOUR LOAD
Read Matthew 11:1–30

Key Verses:

If you are tired from carrying heavy burdens, come to me and I will give you rest. Take the yoke I give you. Put it on your shoulders and learn from me. I am gentle and humble, and you will find rest. This yoke is easy to bear, and this burden is light.
MATTHEW 11:28–30 CEV

Understand:

- *Where can you find true rest?*

- *When have you carried a heavy burden? What was it? Are you carrying one today?*

Apply:

Living in a third-floor apartment can be a real challenge. Trying to carry groceries upstairs is always fun. Usually the third-floor dweller will attempt to carry too many groceries at once. Loading herself down like a pack mule, she ascends the stairs, plastic shopping bag handles digging into her arms. Often an apple or canned good will escape and cause quite a commotion, bumping and bouncing its way back to the first floor.

This scene sounds humorous but is all too familiar when we really think about it. Don't most

Christian women you know go around overloaded? Maybe not with groceries but with all sorts of worries and baggage.

If you are carrying a heavy load, know that God stands ready to help you. You were not created to bear such burdens. He offers you a light load. He tells you to cast your cares on Him because He cares for you (1 Peter 5:7).

Pray:

Lord, thank You that in You I can find true rest. Take my heavy burden. I lay it at Your feet. Please replace it with a light load. Help me to trust You to take care of my worries, guilt, and every other burden I have been trying to carry on my own. In Jesus' name I ask. Amen.

....

....

....

....

....

....

....

....

....

....

THE SAVIOR'S COMING
Read Matthew 24:1–51

Key Verse:

"But about that day or hour no one knows, not even the angels in heaven, nor the Son, but only the Father."
MATTHEW 24:36 NIV

Understand:

- *If the Father, Son, and Holy Spirit are one, then how is it that only the Father knows the time when Jesus will return?*

- *What would you like to be doing when Jesus returns?*

Apply:

We all await the second coming of our Savior, but we do not know the day or the hour it will happen. How is it that even Jesus Himself does not know when He will come back to earth? This is because the Son has submitted to the authority of the Father. It is voluntary subordination.

What will you be doing when Jesus returns? Consider the ways that you bring glory to His name on a daily basis. Do you share the hope you have found in Him? Do you minister to those in need? Do you love those around you? If you are a Christian, you do not need to worry. You are saved and will experience eternal life with Christ. Still, we want to be found serving Him and bringing Him glory rather than dishonor with our lives when He returns.

Pray:

Lord Jesus, sometimes I imagine Your second coming. I look into the sky and picture You coming on the clouds! Help me to be ready and to be found serving You and loving others when You come again. Amen.

THE BREAD AND THE CUP
Read Mark 14:1–72

Key Verse:

While they were eating, He took some bread, and after a blessing He broke it, and gave it to them, and said, "Take it; this is My body."
MARK 14:22 NASB

Understand:

- *What does the bread symbolize when we take communion, or the Lord's Supper? The wine?*

- *How do the disciples disappoint Jesus in the garden? Do you relate more to Jesus or to the disciples in the scenario?*

Apply:

There is something special about taking communion, or the Lord's Supper. It is an ordinance of the Church that comes to us directly from Jesus' command to do this in remembrance of Him. When you take the bread and the cup, do you stop to really ponder their significance?

The bread represents Jesus' body, broken for us on the cross. The cup, or the wine, symbolizes his blood, shed for the forgiveness of sins. The Old Testament law required the spilling of blood. Christ fulfilled that. He was the unblemished Lamb of God, without sin, and it is only through Him that we can stand before a holy God, blameless and righteous.

He died once, for all. It was an amazing sacrifice, and the ordinance of communion should be taken seriously and scripturally.

Help me, Lord, to honor Your memory by taking communion with reverence and respect. Thank You for Your death on the cross that provided a way for me to come before a holy God. Thank You that through You I am found righteous and pure. Amen.

....

....

....

....

....

....

....

....

....

....

....

REMEMBER WHAT JESUS HAS DONE

Read Luke 8:1–56

Key Verses:

After this, Jesus traveled about from one town and village to another, proclaiming the good news of the kingdom of God. The Twelve were with him, and also some women who had been cured of evil spirits and diseases: Mary (called Magdalene) from whom seven demons had come out.
LUKE 8:1–2 NIV

Understand:

- *Jesus has freed you from sin and promised you eternal life. What is your response?*

- *Does your life reflect the magnitude of the gift of salvation?*

Apply:

Mary Magdelene is mentioned fourteen times in the Gospels. Her name heads the list many times when she is mentioned in connection with other women. She journeyed with Jesus. She was there at the foot of the cross as He bled and died. She was there at the empty tomb. Why was this woman so dedicated to the Savior? She remembered what He had done for her.

We are told in Luke's Gospel that Mary of Magdala had been possessed by seven devils. Jesus drove the demons out of her, and she went from demon-possessed to devoted disciple of the Messiah.

Are we so filled with gratitude that we give to God our very best? Do we show up? Do we serve? Do we use our gifts and resources to bring Him glory? Mary Magdelene did. May we see her example as one worthy of following.

Pray:

Dear God, make me so thankful for my salvation that I show up. Just as Mary of Magdala showed up at Your cross and Your tomb, may I follow You closely. Thank You for saving me by grace through faith in Jesus. In His name I pray. Amen.

....
....
....
....
....
....
....
....
....
....

JEHOVAH-JIREH, THE PROVIDER

Read Luke 12:1–59

Key Verse:

"Do not fear, little flock, for it is your Father's good pleasure to give you the kingdom."
LUKE 12:32 NKJV

Understand:

- *What is your greatest concern about the future? Will you surrender it to the Lord today?*

- *Can you name a specific time when God has provided for you, either financially or in another way such as physically or spiritually?*

Apply:

It is comforting to read that Jesus told His disciples not to fear. He called them "little flock." We are part of His flock. If you are a believer in Christ, His promises in Luke 12 ring true for you today just as they did for His followers in that time.

Jesus reminds us that God meets the needs of birds and that we are much more valuable than the birds. He points out that the flowers are nurtured by the hand of God. If God meets the needs of birds and flowers, will He not much more so meet the needs of His children?

Take time to dwell on all the times when God has provided. Rest assured that He will continue to meet your needs day by day. One of His names in scripture is Jehovah-Jireh, which means the Lord will provide!

Pray:

Lord, thank You for reassuring me that You will always provide for my needs. Just as You have shown up time and time again in the past, I know You will continue to do so. Calm my fears about the future, and replace them with utter trust in Jehovah-Jireh, my provider. Amen.

....

....

....

....

....

....

....

....

....

LEAVE IT BEHIND
Read John 4:1–38

Key Verses:

The woman then left her waterpot, went her way into the city, and said to the men, "Come, see a Man who told me all things that I ever did. Could this be the Christ?" Then they went out of the city and came to Him.
JOHN 4:28–30 NKJV

Apply:

- *What proves that the woman at the well believed Jesus was the Messiah?*

- *What important item did the Samaritan woman leave behind when she went to tell others about her encounter with Jesus?*

Understand:

Jesus spoke with a Samaritan woman at Jacob's well. This may not seem like such a big deal to us, but Samaritans and Jews did not associate with one another. Certainly a Jewish man would not be found conversing with a Samaritan woman!

As the conversation unfolded, the woman realized this was no ordinary man. He knew things about her that she had not told Him. He spoke of living water, and He claimed to be the Christ.

In her excitement at having encountered the Messiah, the woman left her water jar and ran into the city to tell others about Jesus. She was, by all practical purposes, the original evangelist!

What is the significance of her leaving the water pot behind? Water was fetched from the well using a clay pot or jar. Water was a necessity for cooking, cleaning, and drinking. What do you consider a necessity that you are willing to lay aside to share Jesus with others?

Pray:

Lord, I cling so tightly to my family and friends. I love the familiarity of home. I even find myself obsessed with material things and social media at times. Please loosen my grip on my "necessities," and make me willing to lay them down to share your good news with those around me. Amen.

....

....

....

....

....

....

....

....

....

FREE IN CHRIST
Read John 8:1–59

Key Verses:

Jesus replied, "Very truly I tell you, everyone who sins is a slave to sin. Now a slave has no permanent place in the family, but a son belongs to it forever. So if the Son sets you free, you will be free indeed."
JOHN 8:34–36 NIV

Understand:

- *How is a sinner freed from sin?*

- *What does it look like for you as a believer to be "free indeed" in today's society?*

Apply:

Jesus' death on the cross paid the wages of our sin. He set us free when we placed our trust in Him to do so. There is no other way by which anyone can be saved except through Him.

We are set free from the sins of our past, and we are set free from sin that easily entangles us. Living in a society that is filled with temptation to sin is not easy, but as a believer, you have the power to overcome temptation through Christ.

Thank your heavenly Father that you are no

longer a slave to sin. Because of Jesus' death for you, you are completely free. You will never again be shackled by a lifestyle of sin. Instead, you will turn in repentance after you have taken your eyes off Him, and He will lead you back to His side. You are saved from sin, and yes, you are free indeed.

Pray:

Thank You, Jesus, for saving me from my sin. Thank You that because of my faith in You as Savior, I can be free indeed! Amen.

....

....

....

....

....

....

....

....

....

....

....

....

....

PERFECT TIMING
Read John 11:1–44

Key Verses:

When Mary reached the place where Jesus was and saw him, she fell at his feet and said, "Lord, if you had been here, my brother would not have died." When Jesus saw her weeping, and the Jews who had come along with her also weeping, he was deeply moved in spirit and troubled. "Where have you laid him?" he asked. "Come and see, Lord," they replied. Jesus wept. Then the Jews said, "See how he loved him!"
JOHN 11:32–36 NIV

Understand:

- *When have you felt that God failed to show up or was too late to help you?*

- *Have you heard it said that God's timing is perfect? What evidence from scripture gives this statement validity?*

Apply:

Mary and Martha grieved the recent loss of their beloved brother Lazarus.

The sisters, known from Luke's Gospel to be different in nature, had one thing in common here. They knew if Jesus had been there sooner, Lazarus would not have died.

This statement, which both Mary and Martha make in the passage, reveals much. They had faith that Jesus could heal. They knew He was the only hope. And neither saw how this story could have a happy ending. Their brother was dead.

Jesus was not late to the scene. The Messiah did not check His watch, realizing too much time had passed. Jesus, as always, was right on time.

A greater miracle than healing took place that day in Bethany. Lazarus rose from the grave after being dead for four days. He came forth at the sound of the Master's voice. And that day the angels in heaven surely rejoiced because many believed.

Pray:

Jesus, when it seems You are taking too long, remind me that Your timing is perfect. You are never too early or too late. You are always right on time. Grant me faith in the waiting and in the times I cannot understand Your ways. Amen.

....
....
....
....
....
....
....
....

THE WAY, THE TRUTH, AND THE LIFE

Read John 14:1–31

Key Verse:

Jesus said to him, "I am the way, and the truth, and the life; no one comes to the Father but through Me."
JOHN 14:6 NASB

Understand:

- *What three things does Jesus claim to be in this verse?*

- *What does it mean that no one "comes to the Father" except through Jesus?*

Apply:

Throughout the Gospel of John, we find Jesus using the statement "I am" seven times. Jesus was bold to use this phrase because the name for God that meant "I AM" was so sacred to the Jews that they would not even utter it. Jesus claimed to be God because He is God. Jesus said "I am the bread of life" (John 6:35 NASB). He also said, "I am the good shepherd" (John 10:11 NASB) and "I am the Light of the world" (John 8:12 NASB).

This powerful "I am" statement in John 14:6

declares that the only way to get to God is through Jesus. Other religions teach that good works will allow people to reach God. Some believe that God is in everything or that humans themselves are God. Christianity alone teaches that Jesus is the only way to the heavenly Father. Take comfort in the fact that you may come into the presence of God because you are a believer in the One who is the way, the truth, and the life: Jesus.

Pray:

Jesus, You are the way, the truth, and the life. I am so thankful to know You as my Savior. Thank You for dying on the cross for my sins, bearing them for me. Thank You for providing a way for me to spend eternity with God. Amen.

....

....

....

....

....

....

....

....

....

BLOTTED OUT
Read Acts 3:1–26

Key Verse:

"Repent therefore and be converted, that your sins may be blotted out, so that times of refreshing may come from the presence of the Lord."
ACTS 3:19 NKJV

Understand:

- *How does knowing that your sins have been blotted out make you feel?*

- *What is the source of the "times of refreshing" mentioned in the key verse for today?*

Apply:

If you are a certain age, you will remember typing on a typewriter before the days of computers. If you made a mistake, it took more than hitting the delete key to take care of the problem. Remember the little strips of whiteout? You had to back up. You had to position that little white strip just perfectly. You had to strike the key again. If everything went perfectly, the error was blotted out and where that erroneous *k* or *m* had stood, there was just white. Pure white. No letter. No mark. Clean. Ready. As if the mistake had never occurred.

This is a weak analogy, but you get the point: your sins have been blotted out. Christ took them upon Himself when He died on the cross. Your sins are washed white as snow. Just like a perfect whiteout situation on that old typewriter, Jesus blotted out your sins. He remembers them no more.

Pray:

Jesus, thank You for blotting out my sin. Forgiveness is oh, so sweet! I am refreshed in Your presence daily. I find strength in Your Word and in quiet meditation. I stand amazed at a Savior who would take my sin upon Himself and die for me. Thank You. Amen.

....

....

....

....

....

....

....

....

....

....

....

HAVE YOU BEEN WITH JESUS?

Read Acts 4:1–37

Key Verse:

Now when they saw the boldness of Peter and John, and perceived that they were uneducated and untrained men, they marveled. And they realized that they had been with Jesus. ACTS 4:13 NKJV

Understand:

- *Do others know that you have been with Jesus?*

- *How do they know, or why are they unsure?*

Apply:

Peter and John had been with Jesus. It was evident. They were warned not to speak of Him, but they said this was not possible. They knew Jesus, and they could not be quieted.

These were blue-collar fishermen called as disciples of Christ. And yet they boldly preached and healed in the name of Christ.

When people examine your life, do they know you are a Christian? Do you stand out as a Christ follower? Do you find ways to bring Jesus into everyday conversations? Or are you more like the teenager who wants her dad to drop her off a block from school so that no one will know she is associated with him?

Consider these things. Dwell upon them. Pray about them. Make changes as needed. You want to be a woman who is known for having "been with Jesus."

Pray:

Lord Jesus, I will live boldly for You. I want to be known as one who walks with You. Examine my heart, Jesus. Point out to me areas where change needs to occur. I am not ashamed of You. I want to be bold like Peter and John. I want to be known as a Christian even if it is not popular in some circles. Amen.

WHILE WE WERE YET SINNERS
Read Romans 5:1–21

Key Verse:

But God showed his great love for us by sending Christ to die for us while we were still sinners.
ROMANS 5:8 NLT

Understand:

- *What state were you in when Christ died for you?*

- *Do you ever feel like you need to "clean up your act" before you can talk to God? Is this accurate?*

Apply:

Christ died for us while we were yet sinners. In other words, He did not wait for us to straighten up and clean up and fess up and do better. We couldn't. We were incapable of living any other way until we met Him. We could not be "better enough" to come before a holy God. We were full of sin and we were in a heap of trouble. We were in need of salvation. And Jesus rescued us.

Remember this the next time you feel too guilty to talk to Jesus, too dirty to come into His presence, or too ashamed to pray. Jesus Christ went to the cross and took on all your sin. He bore the weight of the sin of the entire world. He carried His cross to Calvary. He willingly died while we were yet sinners. There was no other way. It was God's plan from the beginning to redeem His people from sin.

Pray:

Thank You, Jesus. Thank You from the bottom of my heart for dying for me while I was still neck deep in sin. You did not wait for me to clean up my act. You cleaned it up. You who had never sinned took on my sin. You paid a debt You did not owe. I am eternally grateful. Amen.

....

....

....

....

....

....

....

....

....

....

....

....

YOU ARE LOVED
Read Romans 8:1–39

Key Verses:

But in all these things we overwhelmingly conquer through Him who loved us. For I am convinced that neither death, nor life, nor angels, nor principalities, nor things present, nor things to come, nor powers, nor height, nor depth, nor any other created thing, will be able to separate us from the love of God, which is in Christ Jesus our Lord.
ROMANS 8:37–39 NASB

Understand:

- *What can separate the Christian from God's love?*

- *What does it mean that you are more than a conqueror in all things through Christ?*

Apply:

Unconditionally—that is how God loves His children. These verses in Romans provide the Christian with a great deal of peace. Even death is not able to separate you from God's love. Why is this? You will not truly experience death. You have eternal life. To be absent in your current body is to be in the presence of the Lord. So even the moment that you take your final breath on this earth you will not be separated from God!

As you go about your day, remember that God's love surrounds you. He has declared you to be more than a conqueror through Jesus. In other words, in all things—trials, tests, hardships, and even your deepest loss or disappointment—you have the power to overcome.

You are an overcomer, and you are deeply loved. Claim the scripture and walk with your head held high as a daughter of the King.

Pray:

Heavenly Father, Your Word is so rich and full of assurances. Help me to claim them! Thank You for loving me unconditionally and making me more than a conqueror over all things. In Jesus' powerful name I pray. Amen.

....

....

....

....

....

....

....

....

....

....

HOLINESS
Read Romans 12:1–21

Key Verse:

Therefore, I urge you, brothers and sisters, in view of God's mercy, to offer your bodies as a living sacrifice, holy and pleasing to God—this is your true and proper worship.
ROMANS 12:1 NIV

Understand:

- *What is holiness and why is it important?*

- *How does one offer her body as a living sacrifice to God? What does this look like?*

Apply:

Romans 12 is a powerful chapter that admonishes the believer to be humble, to love others, and to seek holiness before God.

As women, it's easy to get caught up in outward appearance. Our society is consumed with style and fashion, exercise and fitness. There is a new diet plan every week it seems! While certainly physical health is important, Romans 12:1 points out that holiness supersedes even physical health.

When you live your life in humility, serving others, using your gifts, and showing love, you please

God. Is it more important that you have the latest hairstyle or fashion trend or that you do what is right and live at peace with those around you? God sees the heart. Seek to be holy. Ask Him to help you.

Pray:

Lord, help me to live out Romans 12 today. Give me the strength to cling to good and to stay away from evil. Strengthen me that I might use my gifts to bring You glory and honor. Help me to seek holiness that I might please You, Father. In Jesus' name I pray. Amen.

....

....

....

....

....

....

....

....

....

....

....

....

DISCERNMENT THROUGH THE SPIRIT

Read 1 Corinthians 2:1–16

Key Verses:

This is what we speak, not in words taught us by human wisdom but in words taught by the Spirit, explaining spiritual realities with Spirit-taught words. The person without the Spirit does not accept the things that come from the Spirit of God but considers them foolishness, and cannot understand them because they are discerned only through the Spirit.

1 Corinthians 2:13–14 NIV

Understand:

- *Who is able to understand things that come from the Spirit of God? Who is not able to accept these things?*

- *What is the difference between these two types of people, and which type are you?*

Apply:

The things of God seem foolish to those who do not have the Holy Spirit. When you accepted Christ, you were sealed with the Holy Spirit. This enables you to understand and apply God's Word and His ways.

Don't be surprised if unbelievers argue with you about the validity of scripture. They are wearing spiritual blinders. They are unable to see or comprehend scripture.

The Holy Spirit is our Comforter and our Counselor. The Holy Spirit enables us to understand and apply God's Word. Praise God that you do not wear a veil that keeps you from taking in His Word. Pray diligently for those you know who have not yet come to know Christ. Their lives depend on the shedding of those spiritual blinders. They need the freedom that comes through the Spirit. They need Jesus.

Heavenly Father, I thank You that I have the Holy Spirit. I am so thankful that I am able to understand Your Word and apply it to my life. It saddens me that so many see spiritual things as foolishness. I pray for repentance in their lives that they might accept Christ and receive the blessings of the Holy Spirit. Amen.

....

....

....

....

....

....

....

....

OLD VS. NEW
Read 2 Corinthians 5:1–21

Key Verse:

Therefore, if anyone is in Christ, the new creation has come:
The old has gone, the new is here!
2 CORINTHIANS 5:17 NIV

Understand:

- *What guilt do you often attempt to hold on to*
  from your past even though Christ has given
  you new life?

- *How are we to regard other believers—based*
  on their past or on their identity in Christ?
  What is our identity in Christ?

Apply:

Our sin was laid on Christ, the only sinless man, the
Son of God. He died for us, once for all, and if we
have trusted in Him as Savior, we are forgiven.

So why do we live weighed down in the muck
and mire of a not-so-pleasant past? Do you find it
hard to fully let go of the sin you committed prior to
asking Jesus to be your Savior?

You are in good company. It's a natural tendency.
Still, we must recognize that we are not the same
anymore. The old person has gone. The new has

come. God sees you not as you were but through a Jesus lens. And through that lens, He sees you as righteous. Don't waste precious energy toting around an unnecessary load of guilt. Lay it down today. Once and for all. And use that energy to spread the Gospel to those who do not yet know the Savior.

Pray:

Lord, lift the burden of guilt I so unnecessarily cling to. Remind me that through Jesus Christ, I am seen as righteous, forgiven, free, and best of all—new! I am not the woman I was before I came to Christ. The old has gone, and the new has come. Amen.

....

....

....

....

....

....

....

....

....

....

....

....

A CHEERFUL GIVER
Read 2 Corinthians 9:1–15

Key Verse:

So let each one give as he purposes in his heart, not grudgingly or of necessity; for God loves a cheerful giver.
2 CORINTHIANS 9:7 NKJV

Understand:

- *When you give, do you do so cheerfully or begrudgingly?*

- *Where do you think your attitude toward giving originated? Does it need any modification or fine-tuning after reading this passage?*

Apply:

Have you read the picture book called *The Giving Tree* by Shel Silverstein? It's about a tree that gives and gives to a young boy. As the boy grows, his needs change. The tree willingly gives shade and its branches to the boy. The boy grows old, and the tree has become just a stump, having given tirelessly and completely. The tree meets his final need by providing a place for the old man to sit and rest awhile.

As the reader, it's tempting to grow angry with

the boy. But in the end, we see that the tree was happy to give to the boy all his life. It found joy in giving.

Are you like the boy or the tree? Are you a taker? Or are you a giver? When you give, do you give with a joyful attitude? Or do you give so that you might be noticed or praised for your act?

Pray:

Heavenly Father, I ask that You reveal to me any change that needs to take place in my heart regarding giving. Whether it is my time, my talents, or my money, I pray that I will give with an open heart and open hands. Make me a cheerful giver, I ask in Jesus' name. Amen.

....

....

....

....

....

....

....

....

....

....

....

ADOPTED BY GOD
Read Galatians 4:1–31

Key Verses:

But when the set time had fully come, God sent his Son, born of a woman, born under the law, to redeem those under the law, that we might receive adoption to sonship.
GALATIANS 4:4–5 NIV

Understand:

- *What is your definition of adoption?*
- *How are believers adopted by God?*

Apply:

You may know a family who chose adoption as a way to expand. Perhaps you yourself were adopted. Adoption is a legal and binding act. It declares one who was not in the family to be part of the family. The adopted individual is given the family's name and all the same rights as a biological child.

God adopted you when you placed your trust in Jesus. You were set free from your sin because Jesus paid the penalty of death for you. You received all the rights of an heir to the kingdom.

The death and resurrection of Jesus happened at just the right time in history. It was God's plan from the beginning to save humanity from sin. Believers have the assurance that they will spend eternity with God the Father. Just as adoptive families celebrate "gotcha day" (the day their child became part of the family), you should celebrate your status as God's beloved child.

Pray:

Heavenly Father, I thank You for Your plan and for Your perfect timing. Thank You for sending Jesus to save me from my sin. I celebrate the knowledge that through Him I have become part of Your family! In Christ's name I pray. Amen.

....

....

....

....

....

....

....

....

....

....

....

....

GOOD WORKS
PLANNED IN ADVANCE
Read Ephesians 2:1–22

Key Verse:

God has made us what we are. In Christ Jesus, God made us to do good works, which God planned in advance for us to live our lives doing.
EPHESIANS 2:10 NCV

Understand:

- *How does Ephesians 2:8–9 say that a believer is saved?*

- *Ephesians 2:10 states that God planned in advance good works for us to do. What have you done in the past year to bring glory to God? The past month? The past week? Today?*

Apply:

How amazing to think that God was making plans for us in advance! The good works that we take part in are part of His design. We are to live our lives bringing glory to our Creator. One way that we do this is through good deeds.

As you go through life, stop to take inventory of your gifts and passions. Talents and preferences were put in you by the One who knit you together in your mother's womb (see Psalm 139:13). When you use them, it doesn't feel like work because you are in your element. You are serving and giving and doing good deeds in your areas of strength.

You may not consider small acts significant, but they are important to God. The Bible mentions that if you even offer someone a cup of cold water, you are doing it unto Him (see Matthew 10:42). What small act will you do today that brings honor to the Father?

Pray:

Lord, it's dangerous to pray for opportunities because I know You will provide them! I long to serve You and please You through my good works. Show me what good works You planned for me in advance so that I might bring glory to You, my God. Amen.

....

....

....

....

....

....

....

....

....

THE LOVE OF CHRIST
Read Ephesians 3:1–21

Key Verses:

That Christ may dwell in your hearts through faith; that you, being rooted and grounded in love, may be able to comprehend with all the saints what is the width and length and depth and height—to know the love of Christ which passes knowledge; that you may be filled with all the fullness of God.
EPHESIANS 3:17–19 NKJV

Understand:

- *Through Jesus we have access to God. What are the words Paul uses when he describes how we may come before God in Ephesians 3:12?*

- *What does it mean that Christ's love for you passes knowledge?*

Apply:

If you are a mother, you have probably worked hard to build confidence in your children. Isn't it your greatest hope that your children know who they are and that they would face the world boldly and with confidence? With the strong roots you give them at home, you've tried to nurture them in such a way that the world cannot shake them.

God loves us in a similar way, yet even far greater. He loves us with an unconditional love that surpasses all knowledge. No one knows a greater love. We are told here in Ephesians that it is very deep and very wide. We are told elsewhere in scripture that nothing is able to separate us from the love of God (see Romans 8:38–39).

Allow God to grow in you a confidence that can take you out into the world. If you are grounded and rooted in Him, nothing can shake you.

Lord, give me boldness and confidence. Help me to know and to feel that I am deeply loved by my Creator God. I have great peace knowing that I will never live one day without Your love, which surpasses all knowledge. In Jesus' name I pray. Amen.

....

....

....

....

....

....

....

....

....

FORGIVE AS YOU HAVE BEEN FORGIVEN

Read Ephesians 4:1–32

Key Verse:

And be kind to one another, tenderhearted, forgiving one another, even as God in Christ forgave you.
EPHESIANS 4:32 NKJV

Understand:

- *Where will you begin practicing this verse: "Let no corrupt word proceed out of your mouth, but what is good for necessary edification, that it may impart grace to the hearers" (Ephesians 4:29 NKJV)?*

- *Compare and contrast the emotions and actions of Ephesians 4:31 with those of Ephesians 4:32. What stands out to you?*

Apply:

Social media resonates every moment of the day with the attitudes the believers of Ephesus were warned against.

Instead of jumping on the world's bandwagon, believing and declaring your right to hold a grudge, listen to the way of Christ. Let it go. Forgive. Jesus hung on a cross and took our sins upon Himself. God forgave us, and we should forgive one another. We have no right to be angry or seek revenge. That is a worldly belief that is in direct opposition to the teachings of Jesus.

Put away evil speaking as the Ephesians were told to do. Let no unwholesome words come from your lips. Instead, be kind. Be loving. Stand out as a follower of Christ.

When the world says you have every right to be angry or bitter, choose forgiveness. Put off malice, and put on tenderness. It will speak volumes to those around you who do not know Christ.

Pray:

God, I thank You for the forgiveness of my many sins that came to me only through Jesus' death. Put in me a gentle heart where once there was a cold, hard one. Replace my desire to speak ill of others. Help me to build them up instead. May I live according to Your ways and not the ways of the world. Amen.

....

....

....

....

....

....

....

AVOID COMPLAINING
Read Philippians 2:1–30

Key Verses:

Do everything without grumbling or arguing, so that you may become blameless and pure, "children of God without fault in a warped and crooked generation."
PHILIPPIANS 2:14–15 NIV

Understand:

- *About what or whom do you complain most regularly?*

- *Are you argumentative? If you are not sure, are you brave enough to ask someone close to you if they consider you an argumentative person?*

Apply:

Paul calls the Philippians to lay down their selfishness in the first part of Philippians 2. Then, in verses 14–15, he instructs them to be found blameless and pure by avoiding complaining and quarreling. It's a tall order when he asks them to "do everything without grumbling or arguing." Everything?! This would mean that even when someone mistreated them, they should not complain. This seems to imply that even when they are clearly right, they need not stir up an argument.

Even though this letter to the church at Philippi was written many years ago, it sure hits home today! As you move about your day today, avoid complaining. Say no to quarreling. See if it makes a difference in how you feel when you lay down your head on your pillow tonight. You can find peace by following this sage advice from the apostle Paul.

Pray:

God, set a guard over my lips today. When I begin to grumble or argue, help me to stop and remember how blessed I am. Give me the mind of Christ. Help me to use my words to encourage rather than discourage those around me. Amen.

....

....

....

....

....

....

....

....

....

....

....

HEAVEN IS MY HOME
Read Philippians 3:1–21

Key Verses:

But our citizenship is in heaven. And we eagerly await a Savior from there, the Lord Jesus Christ, who, by the power that enables him to bring everything under his control, will transform our lowly bodies so that they will be like his glorious body.

Philippians 3:20–21 niv

Understand:

- *What does it mean that your citizenship is in heaven?*

- *What will our bodies be like one day after the return of Jesus?*

Apply:

Do you ever feel like you don't belong here? That's because you don't! As Christ followers, we are aliens in this world. We're just passing through. Our real home is heaven. So if you feel out of place in the culture in which you are stuck, get used to it. Though we are in the world, we are not of it. We are bound for a greater place, and we will dwell there with new bodies that are like that of our Savior.

While we don't know all there is to know of

heaven, we know that our new bodies will be better than our current ones. We know there will be no more tears or death there. We know we will reign forever with our God.

When you don't fit in, it's okay. You are not meant to. Embrace it as homesickness. You are longing for paradise. One day you will feel right at home because you will be with your God in heaven.

Pray:

Lord, there are so many bad things on the news every night. People are hurting one another. This culture is upside down, calling sin okay and persecuting those who seek to be godly. Help me to recognize that I am in this world for a purpose but my real home is heaven. I look forward to the day I can be there with You. Amen.

....

....

....

....

....

....

....

....

....

PRAYING FOR OTHERS
Read Colossians 1:1–29

Key Verse:

Because of this, since the day we heard about you, we have continued praying for you, asking God that you will know fully what he wants. We pray that you will also have great wisdom and understanding in spiritual things.
COLOSSIANS 1:9 NCV

Understand:

- *Who prays for you?*
- *For whom do you pray regularly?*

Apply:

It's important that believers pray for one another. If you have children, you can see God work in their lives in big ways if you begin to pray for them on a regular basis. Pray for God to give them wisdom and guidance. Pray for them to come to know Christ if they have not yet become Christians. Ask God to show them His will and to give them the desire to follow in His ways.

You can also pray for others in your church, your family, and your workplace. We are a family, the body of Christ, and we must lift up one another in prayer. We often forfeit the great power of prayer simply because we don't ask!

Commit today to praying for other Christians. Lift up their needs to the Lord. Ask Him to work in their lives. Then sit back and watch as God works in the lives of those around you!

Pray:

Lord, sometimes I get so busy that I forget to pray. I might lift up a thank-you at mealtimes or an immediate need at the end of the day. Often I drift off to sleep when I'm trying to pray before bed. God, help me to recognize that I am called to pray for other believers and that my prayers truly make a difference. I pause now to lift up to You these special ones who are coming to my mind. . . . (Pray for others specifically by name and need.)

....

....

....

....

....

....

....

....

....

....

....

WHATEVER YOU DO
Read Colossians 3:1–25

Key Verse:

And whatever you do in word or deed, do all in the name of the Lord Jesus, giving thanks to God the Father through Him.
COLOSSIANS 3:17 NKJV

Understand:

- *What all is included in the "whatever" of Colossians 3:17?*

- *Have you ever considered that even the most mundane chores can bring glory to God when done in the right spirit?*

Apply:

Whatever you do. . . That includes a lot of activities, doesn't it? That includes grocery shopping and cleaning the bathrooms, driving all over town as a taxi for your kids, and even walking the dog. How could day-to-day chores such as these bring glory to God? It is not the "what" so much as the "how" that interests God. No matter what you are doing, focus on God. Dwell on the blessing of a home when you are scrubbing its floors. Think about the gift of your children when you are carting them around! Leave your cell phone at home when you walk the dog, and spend that time praying and enjoying God's creation.

Whatever you are doing, do it in the name of Christ and with a grateful heart. This is pleasing to God.

Pray:

God, thank You for the ability to do the mundane chores of my day-to-day life. Thank You for my home and my family and even for the responsibilities You have blessed me with. Help me to honor You in all that I do—no matter how small or insignificant the task may seem. Amen.

....

....

....

....

....

....

....

....

....

....

....

....

GRIEVE DIFFERENTLY
Read 1 Thessalonians 4:11–5:28

Key Verses:

Brothers and sisters, we want you to know about those Christians who have died so you will not be sad, as others who have no hope. We believe that Jesus died and that he rose again. So, because of him, God will raise with Jesus those who have died.

1 THESSALONIANS 4:13–14 NCV

Understand:

- *Who are the dead in Christ, and what does the Bible teach about them?*

- *How should we grieve differently than the world grieves, and why?*

Apply:

As Paul wrote to the Thessalonians, he included some instructions about grief. Believers in Christ in Paul's day, and likewise in the times in which we live, are not to grieve as those who do not know Christ.

Certainly, we are sad when we lose a loved one. But we take comfort in the fact that, if our loved one was a Christian, this is not a real "goodbye," but merely a "see you later." We read in scripture that the dead in Christ shall rise at His second coming.

While there remains some degree of mystery about the second coming of our Savior, we do know that it is clear that because He died and rose again, those who die "in Him" (as Christians) will rise again as well. Their physical bodies will reunite with their spirits, and they will have a new and complete spiritual body at that time.

Rejoice in the fact that those who know Christ will spend eternity with Him. Death has truly "lost its sting" for the Christian!

Pray:

Lord, I am thankful that even though I grieve the loss of Christian brothers and sisters, I do not have to grieve as the world does. I have hope that I will see them again one day. You have promised me this in Your holy Word. In the name of the risen Christ I pray. Amen.

....

....

....

....

....

....

....

....

SUFFERING
Read 2 Thessalonians 1:1–2:17

Key Verses:

Therefore, we ourselves speak proudly of you among the churches of God for your perseverance and faith in the midst of all your persecutions and afflictions which you endure. This is a plain indication of God's righteous judgment so that you will be considered worthy of the kingdom of God, for which indeed you are suffering.
2 THESSALONIANS 1:4–5 NASB

Understand:

- *What is your current affliction or pain?*

- *Have you ever suffered for the kingdom of Christ?*

Apply:

Paul was proud of the Thessalonians for loving one another well and for persevering even through trials and hardships. Do you face pain and hardships in your own life? Do you know what it means to suffer?

Know that God sees your suffering. He is near to the brokenhearted. He binds up your wounds. He loves you with an everlasting love and promises to never let you go. One day He will wipe away every tear from your eyes.

There is a better place. It is heaven, and it is our home. We are but aliens here on this earth, in this fallen world, passing through. Make the most of each day. Relinquish your suffering to God. Trust Him for a brighter tomorrow. He has not left you alone. Even your hardships and trials are serving a purpose.

There will be a new order one day. God has promised us this. He will make all things right again, and there will be no more suffering.

Pray:

Lord, help me to endure my hardships and to maintain a good attitude. Give me the strength I need to persevere. I feel strong some days, but on others I feel so weak. Be my strength. In Jesus' name I pray. Amen.

....

....

....

....

....

....

....

....

....

A GODLY EXAMPLE
Read 2 Timothy 1:1–18

Key Verses:

I remember your true faith. That faith first lived in your grandmother Lois and in your mother Eunice, and I know you now have that same faith. This is why I remind you to keep using the gift God gave you when I laid my hands on you. Now let it grow, as a small flame grows into a fire. God did not give us a spirit that makes us afraid but a spirit of power and love and self-control.

2 Timothy 1:5–7 NCV

Understand:

- *Who lived out their faith before Timothy and inspired him to follow Christ as well?*

- *Who were your examples in the Christian faith? For whom do you serve as a Christian role model?*

Apply:

Timothy grew up learning from his mother and grandmother. They are important enough for Paul to mention them by name in his letter to the young man. Paul states that while the faith first lived in Lois and Eunice, he knows the faith is now Timothy's as well.

A godly example is a great blessing to a young person. Did you follow in the footsteps of a mother or father? A grandparent or other relative? Perhaps you are a first-generation Christian. Did you have a spiritual mentor in a pastor or friend? Everyone needs to see faith modeled and lived out before her.

Do you serve as an example for younger Christians? Perhaps your own children or students? Maybe nieces or nephews look up to you. You may model Christianity for those your own age, your peers. Baby Christians come in all ages!

Seek out a spiritual mentor if you don't already have one, and find a way to mentor younger women in the faith as well. Both are equally important.

Pray:

Father, help me to model the Christian walk for those who are coming along after me. May I be ever aware that I am being watched. Give me grace to live each day in a way that is pleasing to You, and may I serve as a godly example. In Jesus' name I pray. Amen.

....

....

....

....

....

....

ITCHING EARS
Read 2 Timothy 4:1–22

Key Verse:

For a time is coming when people will no longer listen to sound and wholesome teaching. They will follow their own desires and will look for teachers who will tell them whatever their itching ears want to hear.
2 TIMOTHY 4:3 NLT

Understand:

- *Is there a teacher you have heard on TV or the radio whose words did not seem to line up with scripture?*

- *Do you like to be told only what you want to hear, or do you seek truth?*

Apply:

The apostle Paul warns that a time is coming when people will follow their own desires, no longer listen to godly teaching, but instead follow teachers who tell them what they want to hear. Does this sound like the times in which we live?

All you have to do is flip on the TV, step into certain churches, or turn on your car radio. You can hear a message preached in Jesus' name that tells you just about anything you want to hear. Scripture is twisted to fit any situation. Pastors who are filling stadiums are oftentimes preaching a prosperity gospel, full of lies.

Be careful. Test everything with the Word of God. Ask God for discernment. Read and study the Bible. Know it inside and out. Then you will not fall into the trap of following after what your itching ears want to hear. Truth is not always easy, but it is always, always worth seeking.

Pray:

God, I do not want to be told what is easy or sounds good. I want to know truth. Give me the discernment I so desperately need in the times in which I live. Help me to sense when something just doesn't line up with Your holy Word. Fill my mind and heart with Your truth, I ask. Amen.

....

....

....

....

....

....

....

....

....

....

MENTORS AND MENTEES
Read Titus 2:1–15

Key Verses:

In the same way, teach older women to be holy in their behavior, not speaking against others or enslaved to too much wine, but teaching what is good. Then they can teach the young women to love their husbands, to love their children, to be wise and pure, to be good workers at home, to be kind, and to yield to their husbands. Then no one will be able to criticize the teaching God gave us.
Titus 2:3–5 NCV

Understand:

- *Do you know of an example in which an older Christian woman had great influence on a younger Christian woman's life?*

- *Is there a younger Christian woman who you believe could benefit from your mentorship? Is there an older Christian woman from whom you would like to learn?*

Apply:

In scripture, we learn that Paul mentored Timothy. Everyone needs a Paul, someone who has been on their spiritual journey longer than we have. This is a spiritual mentor. Everyone also benefits and grows from serving as a mentor to a younger believer. In essence, you need a Paul and a Timothy, someone to pour into you and someone in whom to invest.

Titus 2 lays out these roles very well and shows us what we can learn from one another. Younger women can learn how to be godly wives, mothers, and workers from women who have gone before them. Older women will continue to grow as they share their wisdom with younger women.

Consider today asking a woman who is further along than you spiritually to take you on as a mentee. Look around also for a younger woman who may benefit from your mentorship.

Pray:

Heavenly Father, please use me in a younger believer's life. Help me to show someone how to live as a godly wife, mother, and worker. Help me also to be open to the advice of a woman who has already experienced more of life than I have. I need a "Paul" and a "Timothy" in my life. Amen.

WELCOME THE STRANGER
Read Hebrews 13:1–25

Key Verse:

Remember to welcome strangers, because some who have done this have welcomed angels without knowing it.
HEBREWS 13:2 NCV

Understand:

- *How do you welcome the stranger? What does this look like in your life?*

- *How might someone act differently if he or she were aware that a stranger was indeed an angel?*

Apply:

In this day of "stranger danger," it seems unusual to read that we should welcome strangers.

Let's examine what this might look like in your life.

Do you host a community group in the house God has given you? Do you offer missionaries or others in need a room in your home for a short-term or even long-term stay? Do you speak to people when you are in the marketplace and offer a smile? Do you give up the close parking space or the last ice-cold soda so that someone else may enjoy it? Any or all of these could be classified as welcoming the stranger.

You never know when you might be welcoming an angel instead of a mere man. Abraham and Lot are just two men of the Bible who welcomed angels unawares. God rewards those who perform simple acts of kindness. Our heavenly Father says that when we serve even the lowliest among us, we are serving Him (see Matthew 25:40).

Pray:

Father, may I use my gifts and resources to help others. Make me aware of opportunities to welcome the stranger in my own way. Use me, I pray, in Jesus' precious name. Amen.

....

....

....

....

....

....

....

....

....

....

GOOD GIFTS
Read James 1:1–27

Key Verse:

Every good thing given and every perfect gift is from above, coming down from the Father of lights, with whom there is no variation or shifting shadow.
JAMES 1:17 NASB

Understand:

- *From whom do all good gifts come?*

- *What are some of the greatest gifts God has given to you?*

Apply:

Every good thing in your life came straight from the hands of God. Your home, car, and the food that fills your pantry and fridge. . . Your friendships, education, career, and family. . . Your talents, abilities, and even the sunsets you enjoy. . . Look around you today. Thank God for all the good and perfect gifts He has bestowed on you.

If you ever begin to doubt God's love, consider His gifts. If you ever start to wonder why He does not give you something your heart desires, know this: He gives you the gifts that He knows you need. He gives you nothing less than His very best.

God is good, and His gifts are perfect. Take time to marvel at all the gifts in your life. Take time to thank the Father of lights.

Pray:

Father of lights, with whom there is no variation or shifting shadow, You are the same yesterday, today, and tomorrow. You are the Great I Am, the Creator, my Redeemer, my Best Friend. Thank You for all of the good and perfect gifts in my life. I humbly recognize that they are all from You. Amen.

....

....

....

....

....

....

....

....

....

....

....

....

....

....

ACCEPTING HELP
Read James 2:1–26

Key Verses:

A brother or sister in Christ might need clothes or food. If you say to that person, "God be with you! I hope you stay warm and get plenty to eat," but you do not give what that person needs, your words are worth nothing.
JAMES 2:15–16 NCV

Understand:

- *What is the difference between faith with and without works?*

- *Why do you think James says that faith without works is dead?*

Apply:

God loves you. All of you. Not just the spiritual parts. He cares about your physical needs as well. The body of Christ should always be about helping one another.

At times you will need help. You may feel tempted to say, "It's okay, thanks anyway, but I've got this." It may be hard for you to accept help. You may feel that you can do it all in your own strength. This may seem strong. It may feel brave. But in actuality, what you are doing is denying others the opportunity to help you. This robs them of a great blessing.

Remember how good it felt last time you extended a helping hand to someone in need? Be sure that you are also allowing God's people to bless you in your own time of need.

Lord, thank You for showing me that faith must involve works. I am saved by grace, but because of Your amazing grace, I am inspired to do good works so that others may come to know You. Help me also to be willing to accept help. In doing so, I allow others to live out their faith as well. In Jesus' name I pray. Amen.

....

....

....

....

....

....

....

....

....

....

....

THE TONGUE
Read James 3:1–4:17

Key Verses:

With the tongue we praise our Lord and Father, and with it we curse human beings, who have been made in God's likeness. Out of the same mouth come praise and cursing. My brothers and sisters, this should not be.

JAMES 3:9–10 NIV

Understand:

- *How often would you say you complain? Gossip? Speak negatively about someone or even of yourself?*

- *What practical step can you take to begin "taming your tongue" and using your words to bring glory to God?*

Apply:

Remember the old expression "Don't bite the hand that feeds you"? This comes to mind when we read about the tongue in James. How many times each day do we use our words to build others up and to edify the body of Christ? And how many times are we guilty of gossip or of putting others down, perhaps to make ourselves look better?

James points out that the same tongue that

praises God should not then curse mankind, whom He created in His image. This, according to James, would be like both fresh- and salt water flowing from the same spring!

Take inventory today. Catch yourself as you are about to utter those negative words, and use that opportunity instead for positive ones. This will honor God, and at the close of the day you can know that you used your tongue in the way a believer should.

Pray:

Dear God, I ask You to stop me in my tracks today when I begin to use my words to dishonor those around me. I know that by making a conscious choice to "tame my tongue," I am able to bring You glory. In Jesus' name I pray. Amen.

....

....

....

....

....

....

....

....

....

PURCHASED WITH THE BLOOD OF CHRIST

Read 1 Peter 1:1–25

Key Verses:

. . .knowing that you were not redeemed with corruptible things, like silver or gold, from your aimless conduct received by tradition from your fathers, but with the precious blood of Christ, as of a lamb without blemish and without spot.
1 PETER 1:18–19 NKJV

Understand:

- *How is the word* redeem *defined?*

- *How have you, as a Christian, been redeemed by Jesus Christ?*

Apply:

Have you seen movies or heard stories of kidnappers holding their victim for ransom? Imagine if this happened to you! Your family and loved ones would pay any price and give up great sums of money for you to be released. Now imagine that someone would give his life for you.

That is what Jesus did for you. He redeemed you with His blood. The Old Testament law called for the shedding of blood for God to forgive sin. The sacrifice could not be just any animal. There were guidelines and regulations. Jesus, the perfect Lamb of God, took your sin upon Himself and redeemed you.

When Christ redeemed you, He redeemed all of you—not just parts. Your freedom was not purchased with gold or silver. Your life has been bought at a high price—the death of the Son of God. Celebrate this redemption!

Pray:

Thank You, God, for paying the ultimate price to purchase my freedom from sin. You sacrificed Your one and only Son that I might have life and have it to the full. In His holy name I pray. Amen.

....

....

....

....

....

....

....

....

....

....

....

CALLED TO HOLINESS
Read 1 Peter 2:1–25

Key Verse:

People who do not believe are living all around you and might say that you are doing wrong. Live such good lives that they will see the good things you do and will give glory to God on the day when Christ comes again.

1 PETER 2:12 NCV

Understand:

- *Why should believers do good deeds? What is the purpose?*

- *What are you doing that points others to Christ?*

Apply:

A major way that Christians stand out in the world is by living good lives and doing good things. The choices you make regarding clothing, entertainment, and how you spend your money are noticed by those around you. People know that you are a Christian, and when you live a good life before them, you point them to Christ.

It's hard to argue with good results. When people see your children showing respect to others and making good choices, they will wonder what you are doing differently as a mother. When people notice that you support missions or give of your time to minister to others, they will wonder why.

One of the greatest ways to witness to those around you is by living a godly life before them. When others notice the difference in you, you can point them to Jesus. Our good deeds have one purpose—to bring glory to God.

Pray:

God, help me to live in such a way that others are drawn to You. I want everything I do and say to reflect the fact that I am a child of the King. Please help me to set a good example and to live above reproach so that others might glorify You, my Father in heaven. Amen.

....

....

....

....

....

....

....

....

....

A LIFE THAT PERSUADES

Read 1 Peter 3:1–22

Key Verses:

Your husbands will see the pure lives you live with your respect for God. It is not fancy hair, gold jewelry, or fine clothes that should make you beautiful. No, your beauty should come from within you—the beauty of a gentle and quiet spirit that will never be destroyed and is very precious to God.

1 PETER 3:2–4 NCV

Understand:

- *What does this gentle and quiet spirit spoken of in 1 Peter 3 look like? When is it hardest to display?*

- *What benefit is it to your marriage for you to lead a pure life with respect for your God?*

Apply:

In 1 Peter 3, men are encouraged to respect their wives and treat them in an understanding way. They are admonished to do this so that their prayers are not hindered. Wow. That shows how important it is to God for husbands to love their wives.

What about the wife's responsibility? The wife should live in such a way that if her husband is not following God's teachings and he sees her life, he might be persuaded toward God. A pure life. What does that look like? It involves much more than remaining faithful sexually. It involves pure speech and motives as well.

Think about how you live day to day before your husband. Is your life persuasive to him or to others? Would it cause your husband—or, if you are single, perhaps a friend or relative—to want to draw closer to God?

God, I pray that I might truly have a gentle and quiet spirit. I pray for pure lips and a pure heart, that my husband and all those who are close to me might be drawn to You. In Jesus' name I pray. Amen.

....

....

....

....

....

....

....

....

....

....

SUFFER IN HIS NAME
Read 1 Peter 4:1–19

Key Verse:

But if you suffer because you are a Christian, do not be ashamed. Praise God because you wear that name.
1 PETER 4:16 NCV

Understand:

- *First Peter 4 warns believers not to be shocked when trouble comes but to share in the suffering of Christ. Have you ever suffered because you are a Christian?*

- *If you have not suffered due to your beliefs, consider this: Are you living in a way that stands out to the nonbelievers in your midst? Or does your life so blend in with theirs that you are never questioned or mistreated for your faith?*

Apply:

Soldiers wear the uniform of their country. If they die, they are honored to give their lives for the name of their homeland. Are we the same? As believers in Christ, we should stand out as His people. We may meet persecution in our lifetime for following hard after Him. People may not understand choices we make. They may make fun of us or even try to cause us harm.

Whatever persecution you may bear for the name of Christ, you will be rewarded for it in heaven. God sees and records all suffering in the name of Jesus.

If you do not suffer for the sake of Christ, take inventory. Are you living in such a way that you stand out from the crowd? Be sure you are not so well camouflaged that no one would suspect you are a Christian. Stand up and stand out for Jesus. A day is coming when it will be even more difficult to stand firm in the faith.

Pray:

Lord, help me to stand up for You and to stand out for You. I am honored to suffer in Your name. I love You, and I want to be known as one who follows hard after You, the one true God, regardless of the cost. In Jesus' name I pray. Amen.

....

....

....

....

....

....

....

....

LIVE IN THE LIGHT
Read 1 John 1:1–2:29

Key Verse:

But if we live in the light, as God is in the light, we can share fellowship with each other. Then the blood of Jesus, God's Son, cleanses us from every sin.
1 JOHN 1:7 NCV

Understand:

- *What is the opposite of light?*
- *What do you think it means to live in the light versus live in the darkness?*

Apply:

As Christians, we have found the light, but the world around us still dwells in darkness. Darkness comes in many forms, but it is always the opposite of God's best. God is light. He exposes darkness with light.

Those who are spiritually blind walk in darkness. They are on a sinful path. If they had the light, they would turn and take another path—the path that leads to heaven. But as it is, they are on the path to hell.

At times, you may feel as if you are in the dark. Depression may overtake you. You may feel that God has left you. He hasn't. It is at those times that you must rely on the truth of scripture. God has promised never to leave you. He has rescued you from sin and set you on a path of righteousness. Remember in the darkness what you know to be true in the light.

Pray:

Lord, help me always to walk in the light as You are in the light. Keep my heart and mind pure even as I live in the midst of an evil culture that promotes sin. Father, when I feel that I am in the dark, remind me that I am a child of the light. I know You, and I am forever saved from sin and destruction. In the powerful name of Christ I pray. Amen.

....

....

....

....

....

....

....

....

....

....

....

THAT YOU MAY KNOW
Read 1 John 5:1–21

Key Verse:

These things I have written to you who believe in the name of the Son of God, that you may <u>know that you have eternal life,</u> and that you may continue to believe in the name of the Son of God.

1 JOHN 5:13 NKJV

Understand:

- *Do you ever doubt your salvation?*

- *Ephesians 2:8–9 states that we are saved by grace through faith. How does 1 John 5:13 confirm this?*

Apply:

There is no way to predict whether you will be diagnosed with a life-altering disease. We can't know for sure if our houses will flood or if we will lose our jobs. Many things are unknowns.

There is one thing you can be assured of if you have trusted in Jesus Christ as your Savior: the fact that you have eternal life in heaven with God.

First John 5:13 says that we may *know* that we have eternal life. It does not say that we can *hope* or *dream* or *imagine*. It says that we may *know*. This means that you don't ever have to wonder again or doubt that you will truly spend eternity in heaven. It is not about how good you are or aren't. It is a free gift that came to you at the time of your salvation. God doesn't take that gift back!

The next time Satan tempts you to doubt this fact, read 1 John 5:13 again and tell Satan to stay away from you. God wants you to be assured of where you are going!

Pray:

Father, thank You that I don't have to wonder where I will spend eternity. You want me to rest assured in Your promise that I will be with You. Help me to cling to this promise so that I do not waste valuable time worrying. All of that worry is unnecessary! In Jesus' name I pray. Amen.

....

....

....

....

....

....

....

....

....

....

IMITATE THE HEAVENLY FATHER

Read 2 John 1–3

Key Verse:

Beloved, do not imitate what is evil, but what is good. The one who does good is of God; the one who does evil has not seen God.
3 JOHN 11 NASB

Understand:

- *What actions indicate that someone knows God personally? How do you know whether someone is a Christian?*

- *Have you been tempted to "imitate what is evil"? How can you keep from falling into this sort of temptation in the future?*

Apply:

In the book of 3 John, the apostle John encourages the believers to take care of the "brethren" (fellow Christians) and especially if they are strangers.

How do we apply this to our own lives today? Look closely at your gifts and resources. Do you step outside of your own immediate family to meet the needs of the body of Christ? After all, in Christ we are all part of the family of God.

Do you have room in your home, money in your bank account, or an ability that can help others? Is there a widow in your church whose home is in need of repair? Do you know a fellow believer who could use your help getting a job or finding a place to live? You certainly cannot meet the needs of every Christian brother or sister, but you can meet some of them!

This world calls us to imitate evil. When you imitate good instead, you are imitating your heavenly Father.

Pray:

Heavenly Father, may I always imitate good and never evil. I want to bring glory to Your name as I meet the needs of my Christian brothers and sisters. Sometimes I get so busy serving unbelievers and trying to win them for You that I forget I am called to meet the needs of those within the family of God. Give me opportunities to do just that. In Jesus' name I pray. Amen.

....

....

....

....

....

....

....

....

DO NOT GO ON SINNING
Read Jude 1–25

Key Verse:

I say this because some ungodly people have wormed their way into your churches, saying that God's marvelous grace allows us to live immoral lives. The condemnation of such people was recorded long ago, for they have denied our only Master and Lord, Jesus Christ.
JUDE 4 NLT

Understand:

- *Have you ever heard something that you instantly knew did not align with God's Word?*

- *What would you say to someone who said that because of God's grace we can live however we desire?*

Apply:

The author of Jude urgently warns about ungodly people who have "wormed their way" into the churches. He does not want anyone to be led astray by them. These people said that due to God's grace, it was fine to go on sinning. Sin was covered by the grace of God anyway.

What a dangerous way to live! And what

backward thinking! The apostle Paul taught in the book of Romans that our sinful lives were crucified with Christ and we were set free. Romans 6:18 states, "Now you are free from your slavery to sin, and you have become slaves to righteous living."

Are there people in your life who claim to be Christians and yet live a sinful lifestyle? Just as the author of Jude warns the people of his day, be warned. It is often easy to be led astray by such people. You want to surround yourself with friends who point you toward godly living.

Pray:

Lord, please give me the discernment I need to distinguish the godly from the ungodly. I never want to be led astray by those who think of Your grace as a sort of insurance plan, assuring them of forgiveness no matter how they live. I want to honor You and live a godly life. In Jesus' name I pray. Amen.

....

....

....

....

....

....

....

....

NEVER ALONE
Read Revelation 3:1–22

Key Verse:

Here I am! I stand at the door and knock. If anyone hears my voice and opens the door, I will come in and eat with that person, and they with me.
REVELATION 3:20 NIV

Understand:

- *If you are a believer in Christ, are you ever truly alone?*

- *Why do you think Jesus refers to eating with the person who allows Him into his/her heart?*

Apply:

If you have Christ as your Savior, you are never truly alone. On your darkest day and in your loneliest hour, He stands ready to eat with you. Why would He use these words? One might wonder if it's because eating a meal together is an intimate act. We typically eat our meals as a family or with close friends, not strangers. We talk as we eat. It's a time to slow down and spend time with loved ones. It's a shared experience.

Even if there is no one else, there will always

be Christ. He is your Savior and Redeemer, your Friend, your Prince of Peace, and King of Glory. He is always there for you. You are never truly alone.

Christ not only saves you, but He promises to be with you always, never leaving or forsaking you. He comes in and makes His home with you. You are His beloved, and He longs to fellowship with you.

Pray:

Lord Jesus, thank You for coming into my heart. Thank You that I am never really alone because I have You. May I always recognize the great gift of my fellowship with You. Amen.

....

....

....

....

....

....

....

....

....

....

....

....

THE LAMB OF GOD
Read Revelation 5:1–6:17

Key Verses:

And they all sang a new song to the Lamb:
"You are worthy to take the scroll
  and to open its seals,
because you were killed,
  and with the blood of your death you bought people for God
  from every tribe, language, people, and nation.
You made them to be a kingdom of priests for our God,
  and they will rule on the earth."
REVELATION 5:9–10 NCV

Understand:

- *What details stand out to you in the description of the Lamb in Revelation 5?*

- *How did the Lamb (Jesus) purchase people for God?*

Apply:

When John wrote Revelation, he was an old man, probably in his nineties, serving time in prison for incessantly preaching about Jesus. Some believe that God preserved John's life, allowing him to live well into his nineties so that he might receive the Revelation and record it.

Jesus is described in these verses as a lamb who appeared to have been killed. And yet He is very much alive and is declared the only One worthy of opening the scrolls.

These verses also point out that Jesus died for people of every tribe and tongue. It is easy at times to imagine heaven as a place where everyone looks like you and speaks your language. Jesus died for people of all races, cultures, and languages. Heaven will be an amazing place because we will all be together, worshipping our Lord—the only One who is worthy of our praise, the Lamb who was slain for our iniquities.

Pray:

Jesus, You alone are worthy of all the praise and all the glory. You are worthy yesterday, today, and tomorrow. You are the perfect, unblemished Lamb of God, slain that we might have life abundant and eternal. I bow now before Your holiness. I look forward to the day when I will join with those of every tribe and tongue in worship of Your name. Amen.

....

....

....

....

....

....

NO MORE TEARS
Read Revelation 21:1–27

Key Verse:

"He will wipe every tear from their eyes. There will be no more death or mourning or crying or pain, for the old order of things has passed away."
REVELATION 21:4 NIV

Understand:

- *Can you imagine a world without death, mourning, crying, or pain?*

- *What is "the old order of things" that will pass away when Jesus returns and His kingdom is established?*

Apply:

All we have ever known is the old order. The old order is how life has been since the fall of man in the Garden of Eden. But it is not all we will ever know. There is a better day ahead for those who know Jesus.

God is the Alpha and Omega, the beginning and the end, as was declared to the author in his vision of the Revelation.

Even though things may seem hopeless as you battle cancer or live life with a difficult spouse, they are not hopeless. Regardless of how bad things may get in this world, there is another life to come. You will never shed another tear. You will experience no more pain. God Himself shall wipe away the tears from your eyes. He is in control.

Pray:

Lord, this life is hard. I get so discouraged. It seems that as soon as things begin to get easier, the world throws me another curveball. I am so thankful to know that this is not the end of my story. In You I am confident of eternity in a much better place. In Jesus' name I pray. Amen.

....

....

....

....

....

....

....

....

....

....

....

....

STILL ONLY HAVE 5 MINUTES?
TRY THIS!

The 5-Minute Prayer Plan

Many Christians yearn for a dynamic prayer life,
but we often get stuck in a repetitive routine of
prayer. This practical and inspirational guide will
give you new ways to approach prayer with 90
focused 5-minute plans for your daily quiet
time. These prayer plans explore a variety
of life themes great for all ages.

Paperback / 978-1-68322-462-4 / $5.99